# Collectible Enameled Ware:
## American & European

### David T. Pikul & Ellen M. Plante
#### Photography by David T. Pikul

4880 Lower Valley Rd. Atglen, PA 19310 USA

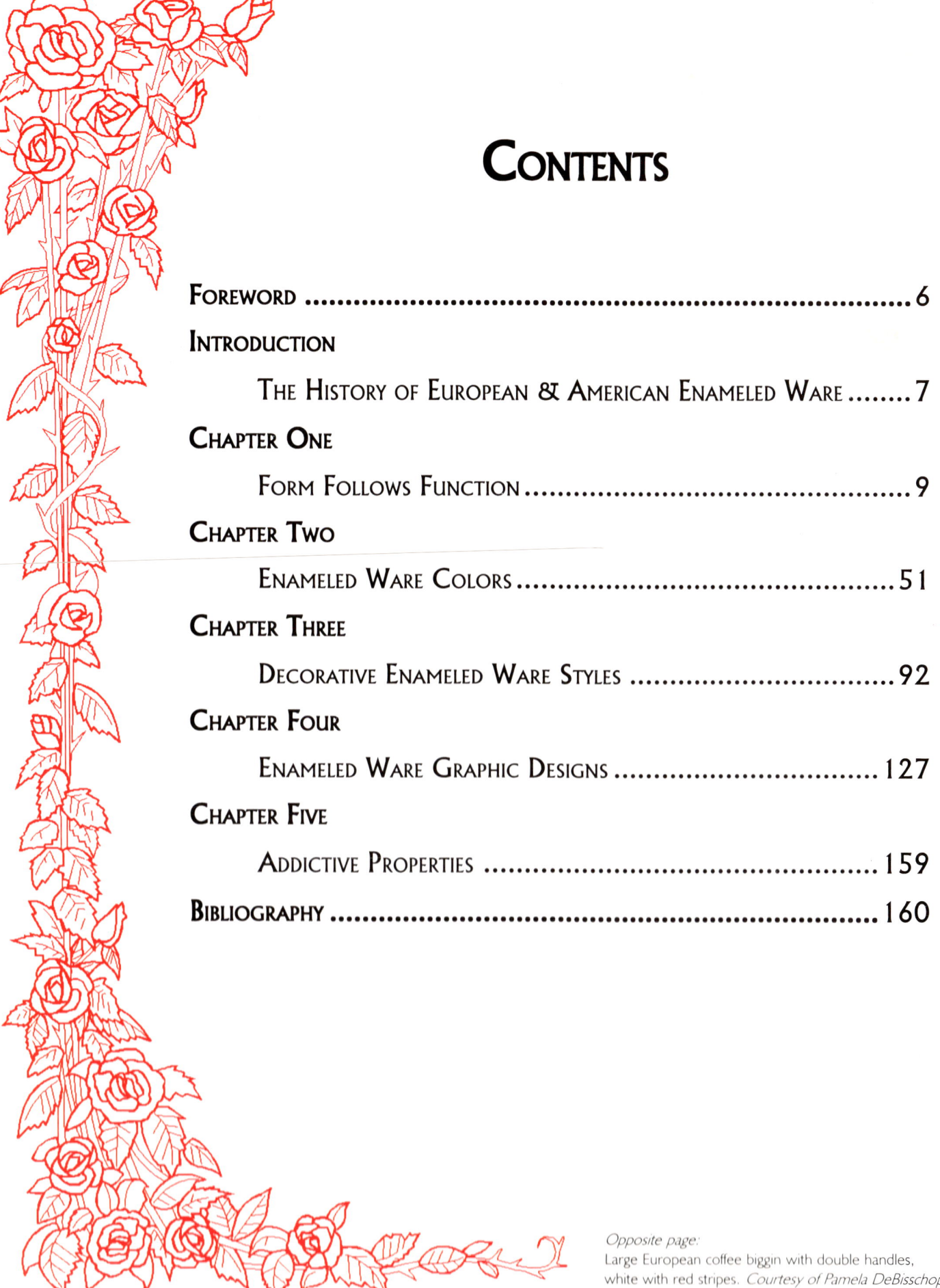

# Contents

**Foreword** .................................................... 6

**Introduction**
    The History of European & American Enameled Ware ........ 7

**Chapter One**
    Form Follows Function .................................... 9

**Chapter Two**
    Enameled Ware Colors .................................... 51

**Chapter Three**
    Decorative Enameled Ware Styles ......................... 92

**Chapter Four**
    Enameled Ware Graphic Designs ......................... 127

**Chapter Five**
    Addictive Properties ................................... 159

**Bibliography** .............................................. 160

*Opposite page:*
Large European coffee biggin with double handles, white with red stripes. *Courtesy of Pamela DeBisschop.*

# FOREWORD

From the authors' viewpoint this work is first and foremost a visual tour of the myriad beautiful pieces of antique enameled ware available for collecting today. It is also, at long last, a celebration of European examples that feature the most striking graphic designs. For far too long European enameled ware has been overlooked in favor of American made pieces by many collectors. But no longer—as dealers and collectors have become more knowledgeable—they've come to realize the artistic merit and quality craftsmanship of old European enameled ware. Hopefully the text that follows will shed light on the subject while the photographs clearly say the rest.

For you, the collector, this may simply be a value guide. Please keep in mind the key word is indeed "guide." As with any antiques and collectibles book that offers prices or value ranges, the figures are not carved in stone. There are far too many variables that affect pricing. In regard to vintage enameled ware, condition and rarity are of primary concern but other factors, such as the area of the country, will also impact pricing. Therefore, the authors assume no responsibility in this regard. Rather, we encourage you to become familiar with enameled ware by visiting antiques shops and shows, researching and reading as much as you can on the subject, and inspecting pieces carefully. Seek out those dealers that specialize in vintage enameled ware and talk with them. They are only too happy to share their enthusiasm and their expertise. A final word, in many instances the values that appear in this book are the asking prices dealers have assigned to their wares in mint or near mint condition.

# Introduction

## The History of European & American Enameled Ware

"How fortunate we are to live in the era of enameled ware..." These words, written over seventy-five years ago, served to advertise the enameled household products manufactured by the Vollrath Manufacturing Company of Wisconsin. For antiques and collectibles enthusiasts, interior design experts, and patrons of lost art forms, living "in the era of enameled ware" still holds true today. The popularity of the colorful, decorative, and utilitarian enameled ware produced in Europe, Great Britain, and the United States since the late 1800s is at an all-time high.

Early on, enameling was inextricably linked to artistry; the ancient Chinese and Egyptians created beautiful masterpieces with highly developed enameling techniques. Throughout the centuries that followed, stunning murals, windows, decorative objects, and jewelry known as cloisonné paid tribute to the artisan's talent and skill.

Fast forward to the late eighteenth century and the quest for improved kitchenware items in Europe resulted in experiments using enamel coatings that actually achieved amazing results. In Germany, a steel mill located in Königsbronn was applying enamel glaze finishes to iron containers as early as 1764 and in Sweden sheet-steel was being enameled by the year 1782. In both countries, work was being done with ordinary copper and iron vessels and various enameling "recipes" were attempted in an effort to perfect a highly durable finish capable of withstanding variations in heat. The French were also endeavoring to develop a similar cookware given the tendency of iron to rust and ceramics, of course, to break. Encouraging success stories in Germany, Sweden, and France slowly gave rise to an industry based on the commercial production of enameled ware for home use and by 1803 the information was being included in general knowledge encyclopedias.

Exactly what was this enameled ware finish that proved cost-effective, sturdy, and decorative, all at the same time? Generally, ordinary iron (and later, sheet-steel) kitchen items were coated with a glass-like porcelain enamel glaze created from a combination of quartz, borax, and feldspar. Additional ingredients were used so the glaze would adhere to the metal base and metallic oxides were added to develop enameled ware colors. This 'mix,' or frit, as it was known, was all-important and its recipe kept very secret; it varied from shop to shop. Manufacturing processes involved cleaning and neutralizing the metal base and then applying anywhere from one to three or four coats of enamel which were individually fired on or baked on in a kiln at high degrees of heat.

Scientists and metallurgists in several studios and factories throughout Europe and Great Britain continued experimental works in regard to enameling through the 1870s and 1880s. Much of the factory work was performed by hand and iron was used as the base metal until advancing technology introduced the equipment and hearths that allowed for the mass-production of sheet-steel. In addition, a Frenchman by the name of Japy invented a stamp press that proved invaluable in the assembly of metal objects. While much of the work could be done by machines at this point, hands-on work and high degrees of skill were still required.

The late nineteenth and early twentieth century period found Germany the most prolific center of enameled ware production in Europe. Companies located in France, Great Britain, Austria, Belgium, Czechoslovakia, Poland, and The Netherlands also turned out notable quantities of the affordable and stylized household goods. Lesser amounts, on the other hand, were produced in Denmark, Finland, Spain, Hungary, Norway, Sweden, Yugoslavia, and the Soviet Union. The most obvious differences among the various European manufacturers were the colors and designs they produced and the graphics they chose to use for lettering and simple to elaborate decorations. Also, certain factories were recognized for their "specialty" items, such as Schweizer and Sons of Schramberg, Germany, noted for their beautiful enameled clock and kitchen scale faces and the highly embellished plates used on the front of coal-burning stoves.

A select listing of prominent European manufacturers that turned out enameled ware for home use, especially in the kitchen, includes Annweiler, Baumann, Bing Werke, Bellino & Company, Becker & Buchardi, and Nahrath Company of Germany; Leopold & Company and Japy Freres & Company of France; B.K. Emaile and Yssel of The Netherlands; and the Riess Brothers of Austria. These firms began manufacturing enameled household goods between 1880 and 1936 and several European shops still continue operations today given the popularity of high-quality enameled cookware items abroad.

In examining the history of European enameled ware, clearly the nineteenth century mind-set that even the most humble household item was worthy of adornment resulted in the production and decoration of utilitarian items bedecked with striking colors and eye-catching graphic designs. This penchant for beautification often had roots with the peasant lifestyle, where daily life was linked to the land and nature was celebrated in numerous ways, including the decoration of simple objects. Such beauty, along with the wide variety of items produced, is what makes antique European enameled ware so desirable and sought-after today.

On the home front, as early as 1848 a patent had been issued in the United States for a metal coating to a man by the name of Charles Stümer. Progress continued and by the late 1800s several American manufacturers were producing enameled goods. They were of course competing with like kitchenware items imported from abroad, but during the early twentieth century World War I put a stop to, or temporarily halted, enameled ware production in several European countries. This allowed U.S. manufacturers to gain a stronghold on the international enameled ware market. This is not to say European manufacturing never recovered; after the war (during the 1920s and 1930s) there were well over 300 firms in Germany alone that produced enameled ware goods. The French had approximately 70 firms involved in the production of enameled ware during the same period and in Czechoslovakia there were close to 50 companies. In Scandinavia (Norway, Sweden, and Denmark), over 15 shops were turning out enameled ware goods. And despite the large volume of enameled ware household goods produced abroad and exported to America during the 1920-1930s period, the industry continued to blossom in the United States.

It all began with European immigrants who brought their hopes, their dreams, and sundry skills to America during the late nineteenth century period. Among them, Jacob J. Vollrath was the first to establish a company producing an enamel finish over cast-iron (1874) and enameled sheet-steel by 1892. His firm, based in Sheboygan, Wisconsin, turned out "Vollrath Ware" kitchen necessities double-coated with a speckled or mottled gray, blue, black, or brown enamel finish.

Lalance and Grosjean of Brooklyn, New York (and later, Long Island, New York), was founded by talented Frenchmen Charles Lalance and Florian Grosjean. They too began producing enameled ware in the 1870s. L&G became well known for the high quality of their mottled "Agate Ware" made with not two, but three durable coatings of enamel.

A third company, the St. Louis Stamping Company of St. Louis, Missouri, was begun by the German Niedringhaus brothers in the 1860s, but their production of enameled ware came later. Eventually the firm became part of a multi-company merger resulting in the formation of the National Enameling & Stamping Company, better known as NESCO.

These companies, along with numerous other smaller manufacturers across the country (approximately 80 located in the United States by the early 1900s), produced enameled kitchen, household, and hospital products through the 1930s. Although they have long since gone out of business or been absorbed by others, their product names have remained popular to this day and collectors will generically refer to enameled ware as "granite ware" or "agate ware." A partial listing of other American firms includes The American Rolling Mill Company, The Bellaire Enamel Company, Canton Stamping and Enameling Company, Republic Stamping and Enameling Company, The Strong Manufacturing Company, and Enterprise Enamel Company, of Ohio; Republic Metalware Company, Iron Clad Manufacturing Company, and Lisk Manufacturing Company, of New York; Baltimore Stamping and Enameling Company of Maryland; Columbian Enameling and Stamping Company, of Indiana; Dover Stamping and Manufacturing, of Massachusetts; Polar Ware Company, of Wisconsin; Manning-Bowman and Company and The New England Enameling Company, of Connecticut; and The Success Enameling and Stamping Company of Missouri.

Enameled cookware, kitchen, and household items remained popular until the late 1930s or so. By the early 1940s, aluminum, oven-to-table cookware, and glass baking dishes had stolen enameled ware's thunder. As the new darlings of the American housewares market, it wasn't long before these modern materials replaced enameled ware in the kitchen. And although enameled ware was once again produced during the 1950s through the 1970s (and is still being produced today in China and Mexico), it is the early, "hands-on" products of the late 1800s-1940 period that have caught the eye of collectors and interior designers. Their form followed function, with magnificent colors, attractive styles, and unsurpassed designs.

## Chapter One
# Form Follows Function

A wide array of enameled products were manufactured for home use between the late 1800s and 1940. Being lightweight and easy to clean made enameled ware an attractive alternative to heavy cast-iron cookware, costly copper cookware, and tin items that had a tendency to rust.

As enameled ware caught on and the market for these utilitarian goods flourished, both here in the United States and abroad, institutions such as hospitals and hotels found the "sanitary" properties of enameled ware (especially white examples) desirable in the war against germs and promoting cleanliness. Household use, however, is our main concern, and while enameled ware is most frequently associated with the kitchen, a variety of pieces were created for use about the house and for the daily toilette. Decorative "hand-painted" and pewter-trimmed enameled ware even made its way into the middle class Victorian dining room.

During the late 1800s and early twentieth century, European and American manufacturers were turning out large quantities of enameled ware intended for use in cooking and baking. Popular items included pots and pans, utensils, measuring pitchers in different sizes, colanders, fish kettles, pie plates, muffin pans, roasters, coffee pots, coffee biggins, tea kettles, tea pots, funnels, cake pans, pudding pans, cake griddles, molds, and tubed cake pans. In addition, dinner plates, mugs, cups and saucers, and tumblers were manufactured for the kitchen table.

These items and many others proved to be affordable as well as practical for everyday use. For example, according to the Fall 1900 *Sears, Roebuck and Company* mail-order catalog, a two-quart "Peerless Enameled Steel" lipped saucepan could be purchased for fourteen cents; a nine-inch pie plate was priced eight cents; a twelve-cup muffin pan was thirty cents; and a "Peerless" soup ladle was only eight cents. At the same time Sears also offered a line called "True Blue Enameled Ware," with a white and dark blue mottled finish. A "True Blue" coffee pot in the two-quart size was priced at fifty-four cents and a four and one-half quart tea kettle was ninety-six cents. Likewise, the 1910 *Montgomery Ward* catalog offered a 14-piece "Enamel Kitchen Outfit" for $1.98. The set included pots, pans, pie plates, kettles, ladles, and a colander. Each piece was advertised as having two coats of enamel in a brown and white mottled finish. And while enameled ware was most certainly affordable, it was also, for the most part, durable. The housewife had to take care, however, not to drop it or handle it roughly for it could chip or craze upon impact. If chips resulted in rusting and small holes, "Mendits" were available for minor repair work. These were metal discs of various sizes which were placed over the hole and attached with a screw.

While the items mentioned above were turned out by both European and American manufacturers there were also enameled goods produced more extensively—or exclusively—

European salt box, 9" tall, cobalt blue with white check design and French lettering. *Courtesy of David T. Pikul, The Chuctanunda Antique Co.* $150-225.

in particular countries due to culinary practices and cultural as well as household customs. The coffee biggin is a perfect example. First invented during the early 1800s by the Frenchman it's named after, enameled ware coffee biggins were produced in large numbers in France and other European nations but on a much smaller scale in the United States were they were referred to simply as French coffee pots. Coffee biggins were, in fact, "dripolators" which included a removable middle section. At its top sat a removable perforated disk and at its bottom was a screen or sock on which ground coffee was placed. Hot water was poured over the disk and allowed to pass through the ground coffee into the pot below. When serving, the filter was usually removed and the lid placed atop the pot. Because filter sections were often discarded when their screens deteriorated, many coffeepots found today are without them and their value decreases accordingly.

Early European examples of the coffee biggin (circa late 1800s) are actually quite tall with some measuring anywhere from 14 to 17" in height. Also, these older examples sported not one, but two handles; a handle was attached to the filter section as well as on the body of the pot. Coffee biggins produced during the early 1900s are typically 10 to 12" tall. Due to the fact that coffee biggins have a goose neck spout, some might be quick to declare them teapots. Actually, coffee biggins as well as coffee pots were typically designed this way. It's interesting to note that French enameled ware coffee biggins were held in such high regard, thanks to their superior construction and beautiful graphic designs, that merchants from other European lands conducted buying trips to France specifically to search out coffee biggins.

Other notable differences in preferred merchandise abound; Europeans routinely outfitted the open shelves in their kitchens with enameled ware canister sets, wall-hung salt boxes

(typically 10" tall) that were kept near the stove for seasoning and tenderizing meat, and the smaller, wall-hung match boxes (7" tall) that served as a handy container for matches used to light the stove. European canister sets were usually comprised of six or more pieces, either of the same dimensions or in graduating sizes (from 7 ½" to 4 ½" tall), for kitchen staples such as flour, sugar, brown sugar, coffee, pasta, rice, spices, tea, chicory, or pepper.

In contrast, japanned tin canisters along with wooden and ceramic salt boxes were more popular in America so very few enameled examples were made here. The limited amount that were produced by United States firms (such as gray enameled ware canisters with screw-on tin lids) hail from the late 1800s period. One only has to examine vintage catalogs or recipe books to note the difference in European and American preferences in this regard. For example, in the 1887 kitchen compendium known as *The White House CookBook*, authors Mrs. F.L. Gillette and Hugo Ziemann offered their readers an exhaustive list of items needed for the properly furnished kitchen and regarding enameled ware, they included 3 kettles, 2 stewpans, 1 teapot, and 1 coffeepot. As for kitchen containers, they advised their readers to invest in 1 large tin pepper box and 1 spice box containing smaller spice boxes (which were wooden or japanned tin). A similar listing in a 1912 women's magazine recommended the American kitchen include a wooden salt box along with 2 covered enameled casseroles and 2 enameled pie plates.

Another item commonly found in European kitchens of the early 1900s was the wall-hung enameled ware utensil rack. Generally measuring 12 to 14" wide by 19" long, these racks were designed with a drip-basin at the bottom and a metal or enamel bar on which could be hung a set of utensils including a ladle, skimmers, and spoons of various size. The utensil rack was conveniently located by the stove, along with the match box and salt box and it was not unusual for European manufacturers to produce these items in matching colors, patterns, or designs.

The European penchant for the convenience of wall-hung containers also included three-cup laundry sets that could be placed nearby where the family wash was done. French wall mounted racks held three cups—one for sable (sand), one for savon (soap), and one for cristaux (baking soda). The sand was used for scouring and the soda for whitening. There are variations in these sets and they can be found with each of the three cups holding a different variety of soaps. German and Dutch sets almost always held sand, soap, and soda and regardless of where they were made, most triple soaps measure 15 to 16" wide. Wall-hung towel racks were also common throughout Europe and included hooks for towels devoted to drying hands, china, cutlery, and glass. These generally measure 12 to 14" long.

Prior to the advent of indoor plumbing both European and American enameled ware manufacturers found a strong market for their merchandise pertaining to the "daily toilette."

*Opposite page:*
American coffee pot, 9" tall, white and pink coloring with floral design and metal trim. *Courtesy of David T. Pikul, The Chuctanunda Antique Co.* $225-275.

European canister set (typically range in size from 4 1/2" to 7 1/2" tall), white with red checkered design and French lettering. *Courtesy of David T. Pikul, The Chuctanunda Antique Co.* $400-500.

Large pitchers with matching basins or bowls were needed for washing and chamber pots and lidded slop buckets with handles were kept handy in the bedroom behind the closed doors of a case piece of furniture called a commode or wash stand. Thus trips to the outdoor privy could be eliminated at night. European manufacturers also turned out larger "body pitchers" used in bathing or fetching water from communal village wells and these body pitchers are usually 14 to 15" tall. Also used in washing or bathing were two-piece lavabo sets which were produced much more extensively abroad. Water tanks with basins beneath them were hung from walls or specially made wooden supports. Water was released by turning a spigot at the base of the tank. Early lavabo sets featured a dispenser with a decorative tear-drop shape and scalloped basin and many examples were adorned with beautiful enameled ware patterns or decorative floral motifs.

Last but not least, small chamber sticks or candlesticks were made available for lighting the way at night by both European and American manufacturers. Candlesticks were made in different shapes; round with scalloped edges, oval, and square. They, too, can be quite decorative or of a singular color.

While antique European enameled ware is highly prized for its stunning graphics and often bold, vibrant colors, American manufacturers of the late nineteenth century produced their own decorative pieces. During the late Victorian era when the middle class dining room was the setting for many a social event, silver-plate and ironstone often substituted for the more costly sterling silver and imported china. Likewise pewter or silver-plate trimmed enameled ware made its way to the handsome dining table. For example, during the 1880s the American manufacturer Manning-Bowman made available lovely "Patent Decorated Pearl Agateware" which boasted a "quadruple silver plate" trim. Among the many items offered

European towel/soap holder, 11" tall, white with floral graphics. *Courtesy of David T. Pikul, The Chuctanunda Antique Co.* $125-165.

were large water servers with matching goblets, caster sets, baking and serving dishes, trays, coffee pots, tea pots, and so on. Ornately adorned and embellished with nature or floral motifs, these metal-trimmed "better wares" rivaled any other fancy tableware available at the time.

Numerous other forms also followed function in regard to vintage enameled ware. Collectors have long been on the look-out for rare or unusual items that were created for household use long ago such as butter churns, stoves, umbrella stands, rolling pins, and water coolers. There are also miniature salesmen's samples and pint-size children's toys to watch for. Germany produced a great deal of enameled ware toys that mirrored their full-size counterparts in regard to the kitchen and the daily toilette.

European teapot, 4" tall, white with blue stripes and a garland of roses design. Marked "B&B." Quite possibly made in Austria. *Courtesy of David T. Pikul, The Chuctanunda Antique Co.* $250-300.

American teapot, 9" tall, cobalt blue with decorative design. Marked "Universal." *Courtesy of Betty Duquet.* $300-375.

American measuring cup, 4" tall, gray mottled. Marked "Agate Mfg. Co." *Courtesy of Betty Duquet.* $200-250.

European coffee biggin, 10 1/2" tall, white with floral graphic design. *Courtesy of David T. Pikul, The Chuctanunda Antique Co.* $275-325.

American coffee pot, 9" tall, cobalt blue and white swirl with metal trim. *Courtesy of Betty Duquet.* $350-400.

Amercan flame tamer, 6 1/2" size, marked "Damar Products, Newark, N.J." *Courtesy of Betty Duquet.* $75-95.

European coffee bean roaster. *Courtesy of David T. Pikul, The Chuctanunda Antique Co.* $200-275.

*Opposite page:*
American gas iron, 9" long, baby blue enameled body with painted wood handle. *Courtesy of Betty Duquet.* $95-125.

European salt box (typically 10" tall), white with Dutch windmill scene and English lettering. *Courtesy of Betty Duquet.* $175-225.

European bread box, 14" long, rare red with floral design and German lettering that translates into "Give us this day our daily bread." *Courtesy of David T. Pikul, The Chuctanunda Antique Co.* $400-500.

European coffee biggin, 9" tall, wide red and white stripes with petit floral graphic design. *Courtesy of David T. Pikul, The Chuctanunda Antique Co.* $200-300.

American teapot, 10" tall, gray mottled with metal trim. *Courtesy of Betty Duquet.* $275-300.

Enameled lid rack holding an assortment of blue American pot lids. *Courtesy of Betty Duquet.* Lid rack $125-200; lids $20-25 each.

European pitcher, 11" tall and wall-hung containers for potholders and onions. White with pansy floral design and German lettering. *Courtesy of David T. Pikul, The Chuctanunda Antique Co.* $150-200 each.

American berry bucket, 8" tall, cobalt blue and white swirl with metal lid and handle. *Courtesy of David T. Pikul, The Chuctanunda Antique Co.* $275-350.

Personalized European plates and cups, white with red trim and floral design. *Courtesy of Pam DeBisschop.*

Large European coffee biggin with double handles, circa 1880s, white with blue graphic design. *Courtesy of David T. Pikul, The Chuctanunda Antique Co.* $350-500.

American colander, 4 1/2" tall, blue and white swirl. *Courtesy of David T. Pikul, The Chuctanunda Antique Co.* $250-325.

European canister set in a rare hexagonal shape, blue with white checks and French lettering. *Courtesy of David T. Pikul, The Chuctanunda Antique Co.* $450-600.

European coffee biggin, 10" tall, red with black and white diamond graphic design. *Courtesy of David T. Pikul, The Chuctanunda Antique Co.* $350-500.

European lavabo (tanks typically 13" tall), rare Art Deco graphic design. *Courtesy of David T. Pikul, The Chuctanunda Antique Co.* $450-600.

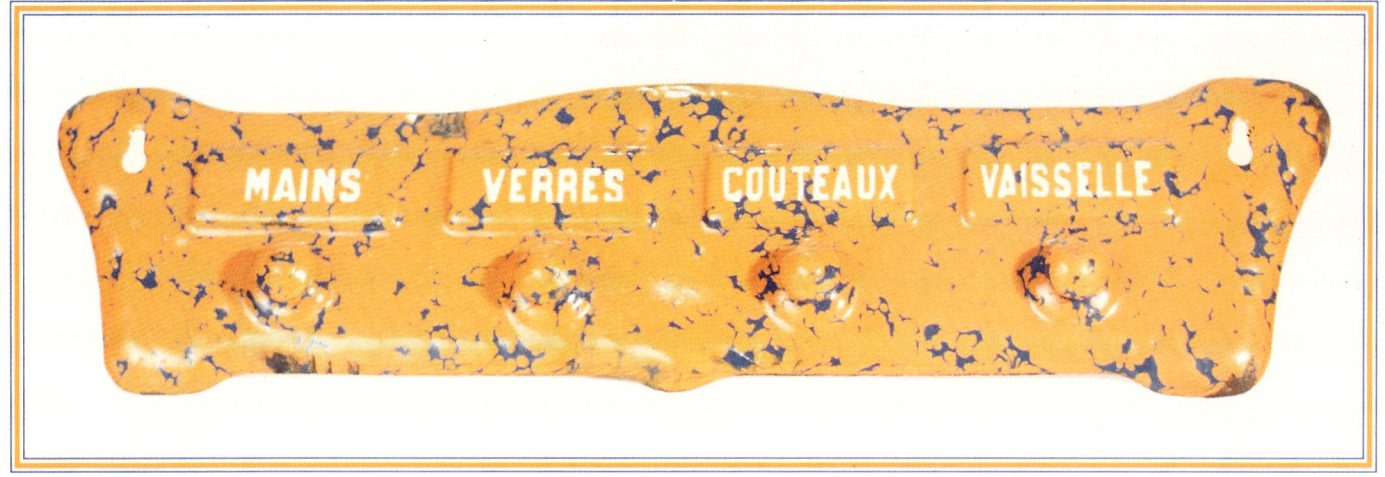

European wall-hung towel rack (typically 12" to 14" long), "end of the day" coloring (refers to three or more colors used in the enameling process). French lettering indicates hooks for hand, glass, cutlery, and china towels. *Courtesy of Susan Curran, Snow Leopard Antiques.* $150-200.

European footed pitcher, 9 3/4" tall, chicken wire pattern. *Courtesy of Susan Curran, Snow Leopard Antiques.* $200-300.

European coffee biggin, 10 1/2" tall, rare pink with floral graphics. *Courtesy of Susan Curran, Snow Leopard Antiques.* $400-475.

21

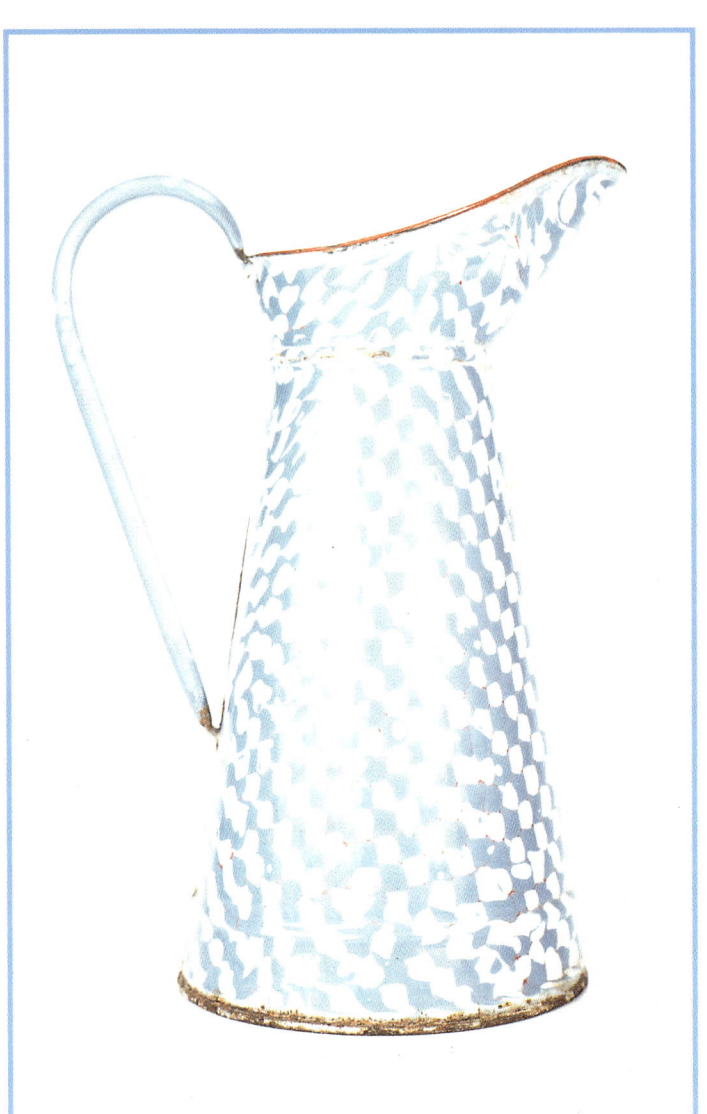

European body pitcher, 15" tall, rare blue and white droopy check pattern with red trim. *Courtesy of Susan Curran, Snow Leopard Antiques.* $350-500.

American double boiler, 8" tall, cobalt blue and white swirl. *Courtesy of David T. Pikul, The Chuctanunda Antique Co.* $400-500.

European wall-hung triple-cup laundry set (typically 15" long), chicken wire pattern with German lettering for soap, sand, and soda. *Courtesy of Susan Curran, Snow Leopard Antiques.* $375-425.

European wall-hung flour box, white with blue windmill scene, wooden lid, and German lettering. *Courtesy of Susan Curran, Snow Leopard Antiques.* $225-300.

European wall-hung brush holder, 15" tall, chicken wire pattern with German lettering. *Courtesy of Susan Curran, Snow Leopard Antiques.* $300-375.

European coffee biggin, 8" tall, yellow with black graphic design. *Courtesy of David T. Pikul, The Chuctanunda Antique Co.* $250-325.

American muffin pan, 7 1/2" x 14" with rare cobalt blue and white swirl pattern. *Courtesy of David T. Pikul, The Chuctanunda Antique Co.* $500-600.

European pitcher, 12" tall, blue and white marbled with an unusual flared handle. *Courtesy of Pamela DeBisschop.* $275-325.

European body pitcher, 15" tall, brown and white air-brushed stencil design. *Courtesy of Susan Curran, Snow Leopard Antiques.* $300-400.

European coffee pot, 9" tall, white with floral graphic design and wooden handle. *Courtesy of David T. Pikul, The Chuctanunda Antique Co.* $150-200.

European measuring pitcher, 6" tall, yellow and white droopy check design with red trim. *Courtesy of Susan Curran, Snow Leopard Antiques.* $200-300.

European pans in assorted sizes, light blue and white striping with garland of roses design. *Courtesy of David T. Pikul, The Chuctanunda Antique Co.* $275-325 the set.

*Above:* European syrup pitcher, 5" tall, light blue with decorative figures in design. *Courtesy of David T. Pikul, The Chuctanunda Antique Co.* $175-225.

*Right:* American vaporizer, 7" tall, cobalt blue. *Courtesy of Betty Duquet.* $60-75.

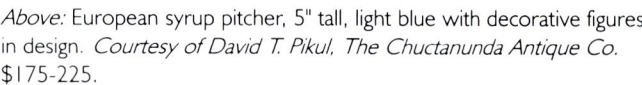

European wall-hung triple-soap laundry set, white with ornate German lettering in blue for sand, soda, and soap. *Courtesy of Betty Duquet.* $175-225.

American utensils, blue and white with black handles. *Courtesy of Betty Duquet.* $65-95 each.

American lidded pot, 4 1/2" tall, blue and white shaded "Blue belle Ware." *Courtesy of Betty Duquet.* $75-125.

European wall-hung potholder container, blue and white chicken wire pattern, German lettering. *Courtesy of Betty Duquet.* $150-185.

Clock, origin unknown but possibly German, 10" size, white with blue graphic designs. *Courtesy of Betty Duquet.* $150-175.

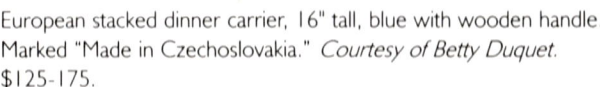

European stacked dinner carrier, 16" tall, blue with wooden handle. Marked "Made in Czechoslovakia." *Courtesy of Betty Duquet.* $125-175.

*Right:* European gas can, 9" tall, white with petit blue floral graphic design. *Courtesy of Susan Curran, Snow Leopard Antiques.* $225-300.

*Opposite page:*
American casserole, 6" tall, blue and white swirl with unusual ribbed lid. *Courtesy of David T. Pikul, The Chuctanunda Antique Co.* $275-350.

European salt box, white with blue shading, floral graphics, wooden lid, and French lettering. *Courtesy of David T. Pikul, The Chuctanunda Antique Co.* $200-250.

29

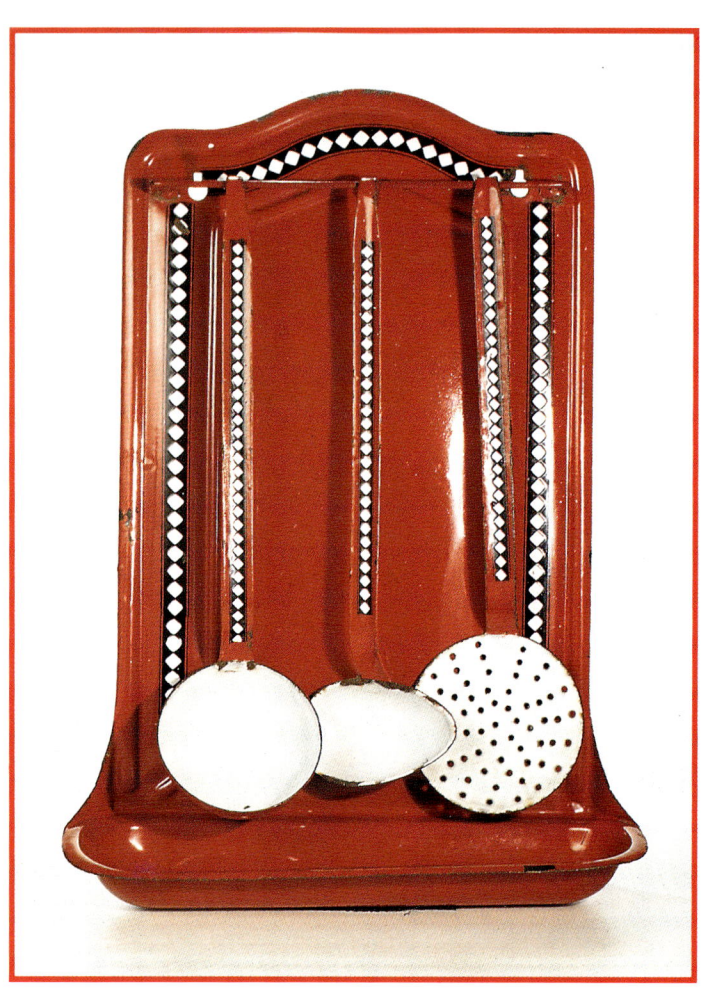

European wall-hung utensil rack (typically 12 to 14" wide by 19" long) with matching utensils. Red with black and white graphic design. *Courtesy of David T. Pikul, The Chuctanunda Antique Co.* $300-375.

European bread box, white with blue windmill scene. *Courtesy of Susan Curran, Snow Leopard Antiques.* $250-325.

European footed tray, 14" size, green with raised floral graphic design. *Courtesy of David T. Pikul, The Chuctanunda Antique Co.* $225-275.

*Right:* European irrigator, 9" tall, white with blue floral and leaf design. *Courtesy of David T. Pikul, The Chuctanunda Antique Co.* $275-350.

Large European coffee biggin with double handles, white with blue graphic design, circa late 1800s. *Courtesy of David T. Pikul, The Chuctanunda Antique Co.* $400-500.

European canister set, red with red and white checkered design and French lettering. *Courtesy of David T. Pikul, The Chuctanunda Antique Co.* $400-500.

European coffee biggin with mid-section removed to show sock that acted as a filter. Blue with white diamond design. *Courtesy of David T. Pikul, The Chuctanunda Antique Co.* $250-300.

American cream pail, 7" tall, blue and white swirl with metal lid and wooden handle. *Courtesy of David T. Pikul, The Chuctanunda Antique Co.* $275-350.

*Above:* European pots in graduating sizes, yellow with white bands and red trim. *Courtesy of David T. Pikul, The Chuctanunda Antique Co.* $120-200 for the set.

*Right:* European wall-hung match box (typically 7" tall), blue with French lettering. *Courtesy of Stan & Mary Ann Szambelan.* $150-200.

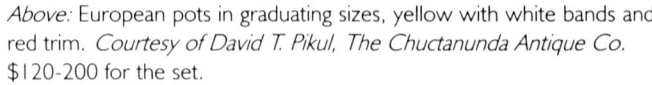

Matching European body pitcher, basin, and flared-rim pitcher with Art Nouveau stylized floral design. Blue and pink shaded. *Courtesy of David T. Pikul, The Chuctanunda Antique Co.* $600-700 for the set.

European canister set, red and white striped shading with decorative French script. *Courtesy of David T. Pikul, The Chuctanunda Antique Co.* $500-600.

American footed colander, 8" tall, blue and white marbled with black handles. *Courtesy of Tom & Lorraine Zavorskas, Cobweb Corner Antiques.* $150-200.

European enamel over cast-iron vase, 6" tall, gray. *Courtesy of Stephen Smith, Foundation Antiques.* $75-125.

European body pitcher and covered chamber pail, rare octagonal shape, white with floral graphics and gilt trim. *Courtesy of David T. Pikul, The Chuctanunda Antique Co.* $700-800 for the pair.

American cake carrier, 13" diameter, cream with nature-inspired graphics. *Courtesy of Tom & Lorraine Zavorskas, Cobweb Corner Antiques.* $100-150.

European canisters (Czechoslovakian), rare pink color with raised floral graphics and white lettering. *Courtesy of David T. Pikul, The Chuctanunda Antique Co.* $300-400 for the pair.

American crumb tray, 9" long, "end of the day" color pattern. *Courtesy of Tom & Lorraine Zavorskas, Cobweb Corner Antiques.* $375-425.

European trivet, 6" size, Eiffel Tower cast design. *Courtesy of Stephen Smith, Foundation Antiques.* $60-75.

European serving tray, 16" size, red with figural graphics. *Courtesy of Tom & Lorraine Zavorskas, Cobweb Corner Antiques.* $100-125.

37

American wall-hung match dispenser, 5" tall, gray mottled. *Courtesy of Stephen Smith, Foundation Antiques.* $150-225.

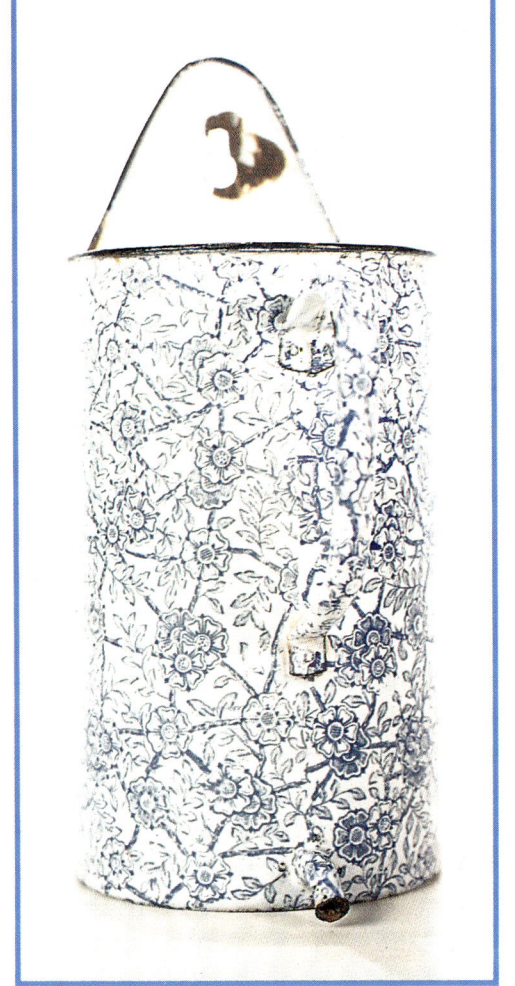

European bouillon pot with a metal screw-lid, 8" tall, white and blue veined "snow on the mountain," rare item. *Courtesy of Stephen Smith, Foundation Antiques.* $400-450.

European irrigator, 10 1/2" tall, beautiful all-over blue and white graphic design. *Courtesy of David T. Pikul, The Chuctanunda Antique Co.* $200-300.

European colander, 16" long, red and white striped shading. *Courtesy of Stan & MaryAnn Szambelan.* $150-200.

European enamel over cast-iron vase, 4" tall, gray. *Courtesy of Stephen Smith, Foundation Antiques.* $125-175.

European trivet, 9" size, cast and stylized nature design. *Courtesy of Stephen Smith, Foundation Antiques.* $125-175.

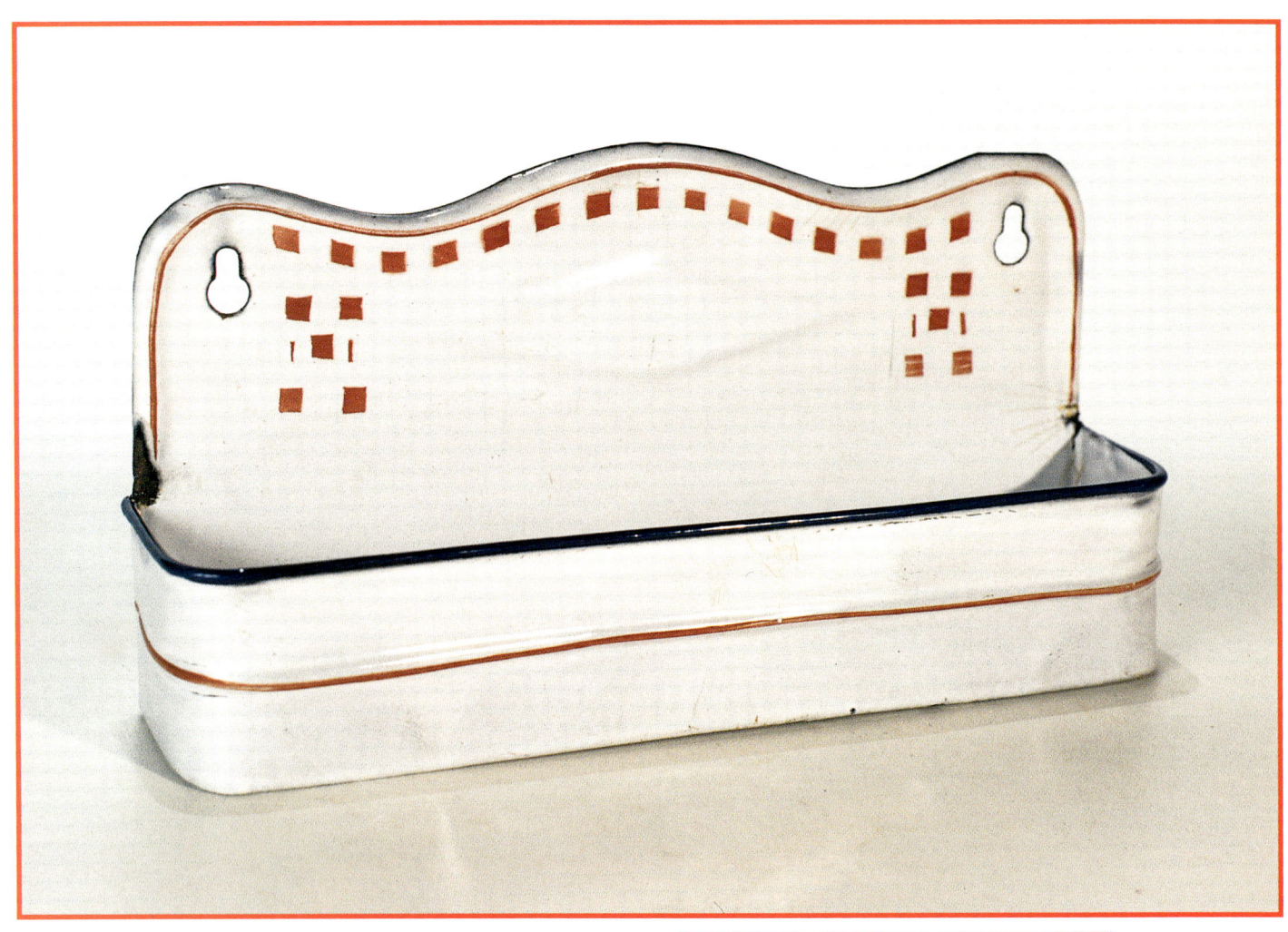

European comb case, 12" long, white with red checks and trim. *Courtesy of David T. Pikul, The Chuctanunda Antique Co.* $175-225.

European vase, 8" tall, striking petite floral design. *Courtesy of Tom & Lorraine Zavorskas, Cobweb Corner Antiques.* $100-150.

European pitcher with flared rim and matching basin, white with red checkered design. *Courtesy of Pamela DeBisschop.*

European footed warming tray, white with metal trim. *Courtesy of Stephen Smith, Foundation Antiques.* $300-400.

European chamber pail with lid, blue and white droopy check, wooden handle. *Courtesy of David T. Pikul, The Chuctanunda Antique Co.* $250-300.

European teapot, 5" tall, pale blue with floral design, marked "GBN Bavaria." *Courtesy of David T. Pikul, The Chuctanunda Antique Co.* $100-200.

*Below:* European kerosene lamp, 7 1/2" tall, white. *Courtesy of Stephen Smith, Foundation Antiques.* $160-180.

European wall-hung match box, large yellow and white mottled with black French lettering. *Courtesy of David T. Pikul, The Chuctanunda Antique Co.* $150-200.

American chaffing dish, white with metal trim, marked "Manning-Bowman Company." *Courtesy of Tom & Lorraine Zavorskas, Cobweb Corner Antiques.* $400-450.

American muffin pan, 16" size, gray mottled. *Courtesy of Stan & MaryAnn Szambelan.* $125-175.

*Above:* American double boiler, 8" tall, black and white swirl with metal lid. Marked "Ebony Ware." *Courtesy of Tom & Lorraine Zavorskas, Cobweb Corner Antiques.* $225- 275.

*Left:* European utensil rack, rare yellow coloring with striped design. *Courtesy of David T. Pikul, The Chuctanunda Antique Co.* $250-300.

*Below:* American fish boiler, 21" long, white with black trim. *Courtesy of Tom & Lorainne Zavorskas.* $150-200.

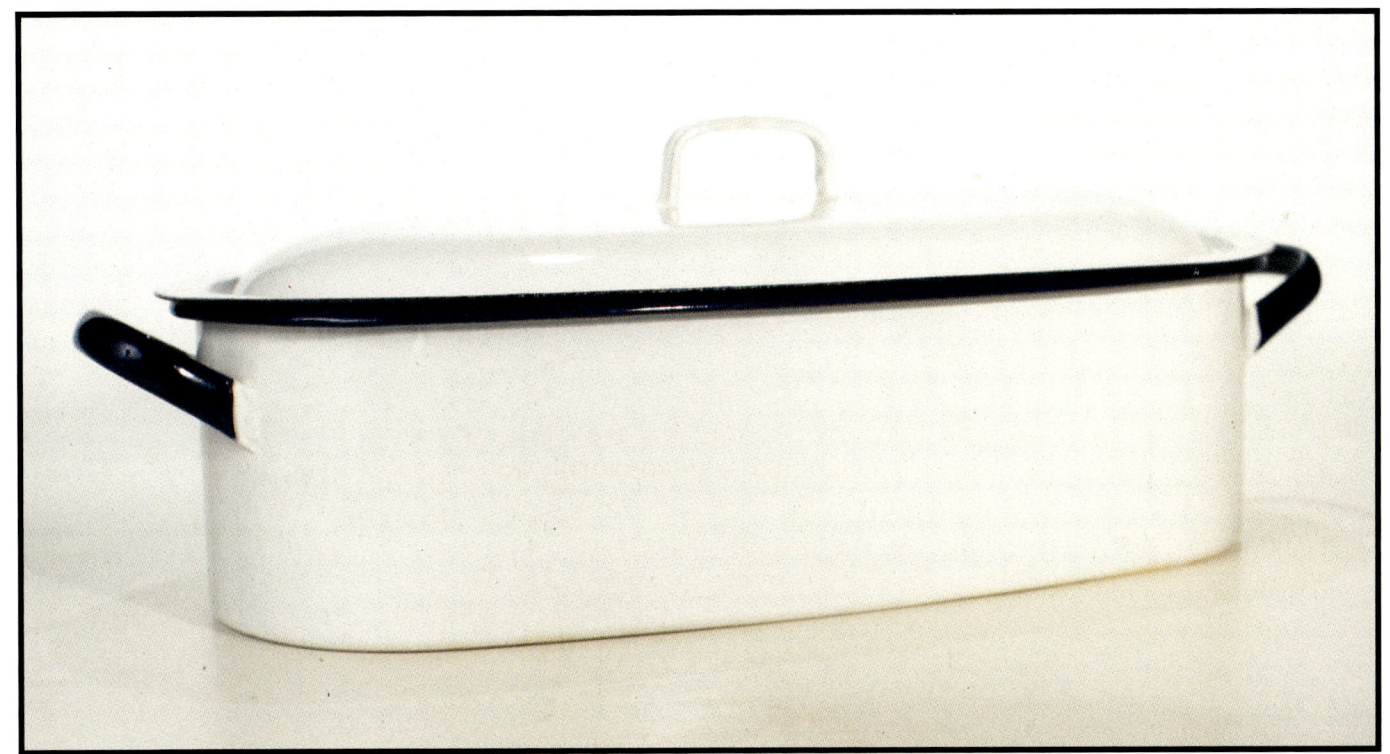

European body pitcher, 15" tall, white with pink and green shading and floral graphic design. *Courtesy of David T. Pikul, The Chuctanunda Antique Co.* $250-325.

American cup and saucer, gray mottled. *Courtesy of Tom & Lorraine Zavorskas, Cobweb Corner Antiques.* $50-75.

*Right:* American advertising item, 5 3/4" tall, likely used as a premium item. *Courtesy of Tom & Lorraine Zavorskas, Cobweb Corner Antiques.* $200-300.

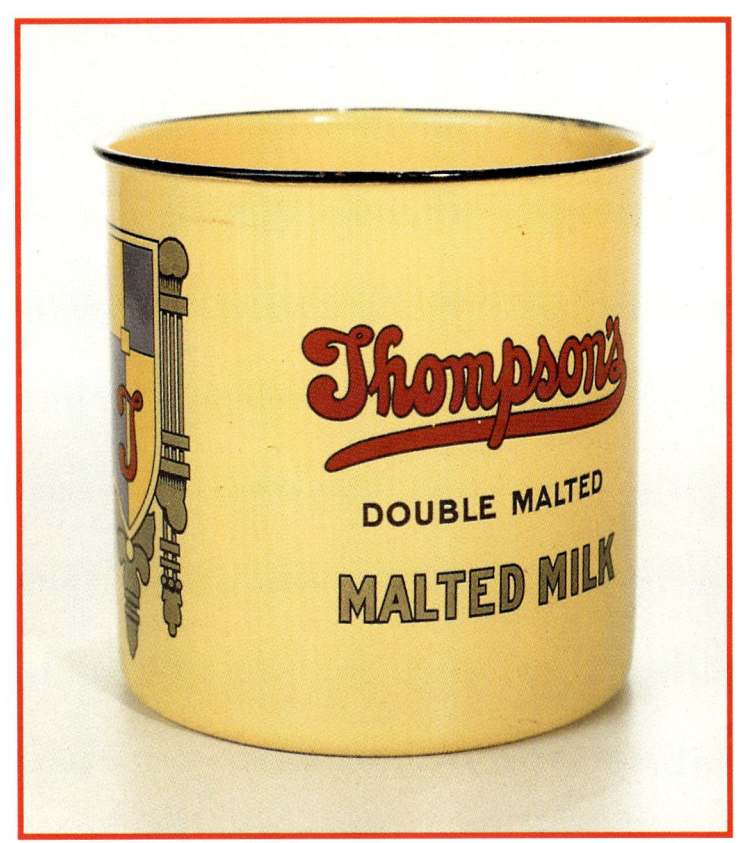

English leech pot, 10" tall, white. Rare item to keep leeches used in medical treatment during late 1800s. *Courtesy of Stephen Smith, Foundation Antiques.* $400-500.

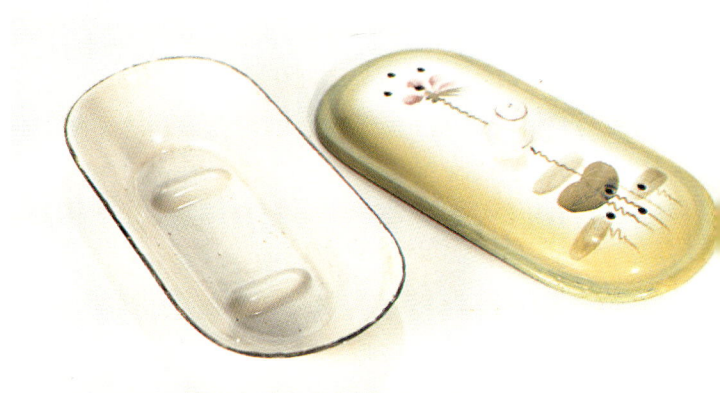

European toothbrush or comb holder, 10" long, white and green shading with graphic design. *Courtesy of David T. Pikul, The Chuctanunda Antique Co.* $150-200.

European coffee carrier, 9" tall, rare orange and blue color combination. *Courtesy of Susan Curran, Snow Leopard Antiques.* $250-300.

European umbrella stand, 19 1/2" tall, rare combination of a brown and white mottled pattern with a floral graphic design. *Courtesy of David T. Pikul, The Chuctanunda Antique Co.* $375-500.

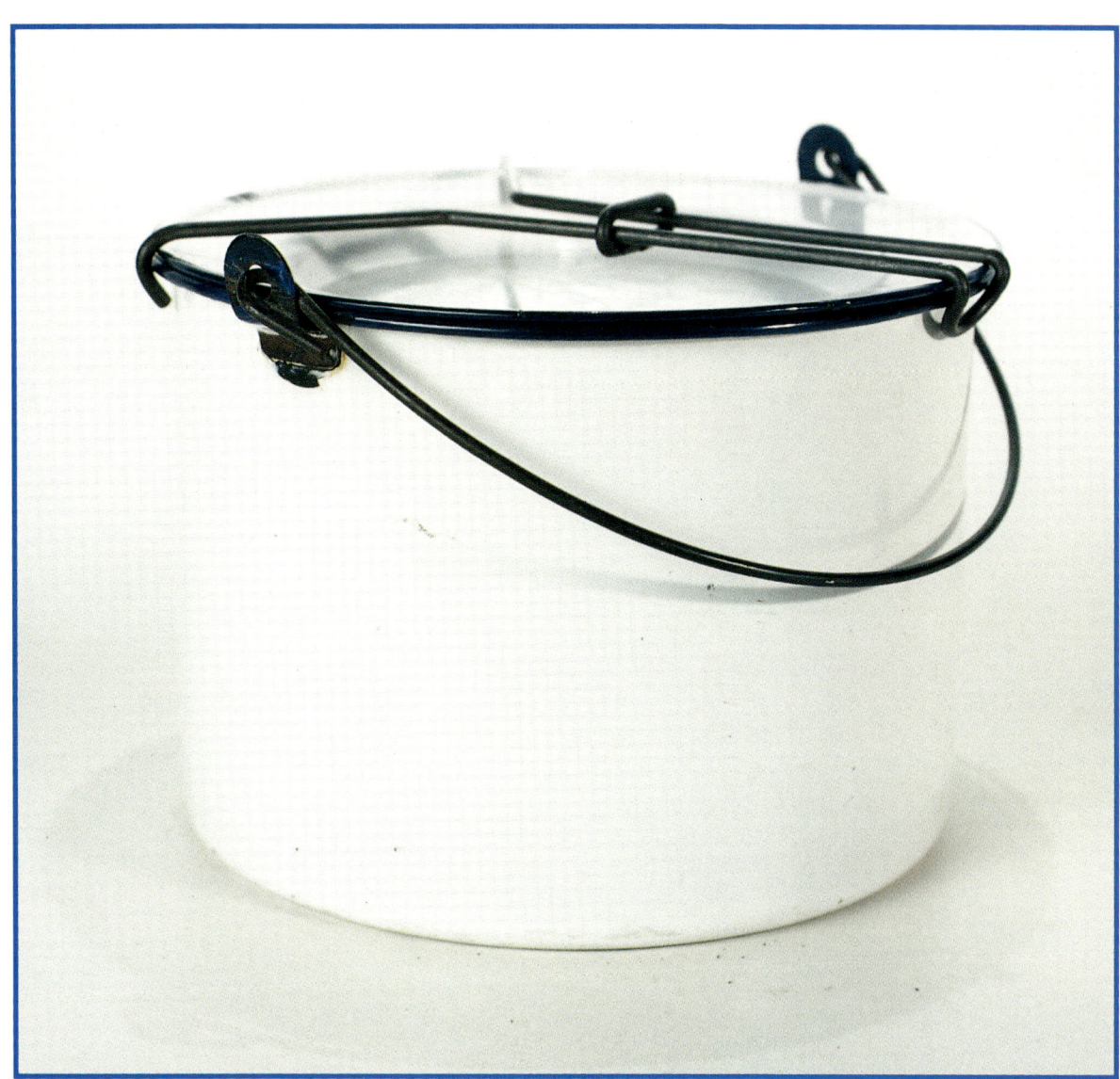

American picnic set (container seen here), 10" size, white with black trim and metal latch and handle. *Courtesy of David T. Pikul, The Chuctanunda Antique Co.* See next photo for complete set.

*Below:* American picnic set including plates, bowls, and cups. All can be stored in matching picnic container. $125-200.

49

European wall-hung soap dish with red and white checkered design. *Courtesy of David T. Pikul, The Chuctanunda Antique Co.* $75-125.

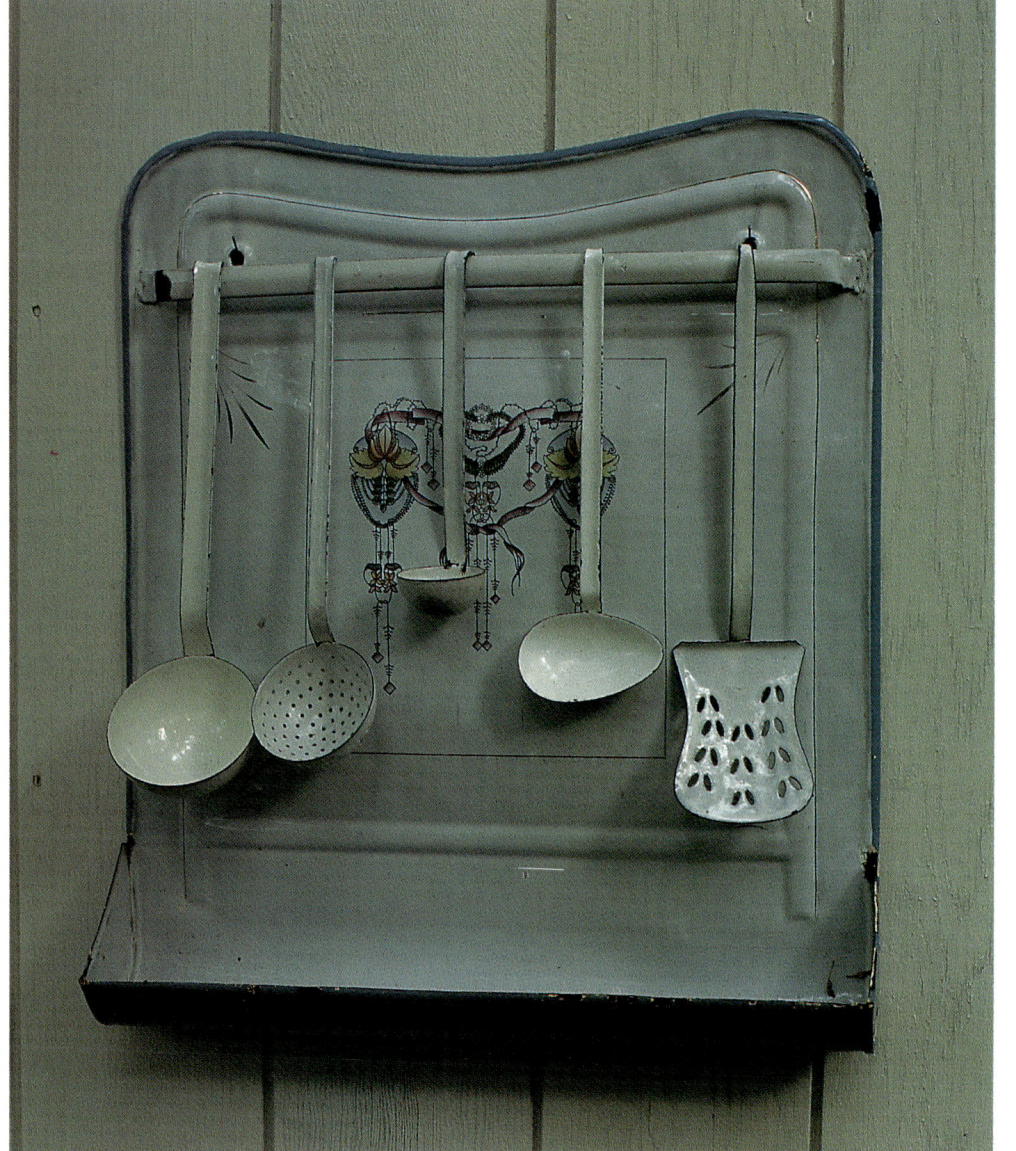

European double lunch pail, gray mottled. *Courtesy of David T. Pikul, The Chuctanunda Antique Co.* $200-275.

European utensil rack with tools, rare hotel size, blue with stylized graphic design. *Courtesy of David T. Pikul, The Chuctanunda Antique Co.* $500-700.

## Chapter Two
# Enameled Ware Colors

One of the most appealing qualities of vintage enameled ware is the wide variety of colors that made their way into the production process. Indeed, color is the determining factor for many a collector in their efforts to amass an impressive collection of these utilitarian household items.

The enameled ware produced early on in European countries was often a plain white, not due to cost factors, but rather the desire to imitate more expensive and luxurious ceramic goods (especially toilet items). In many instances a trim color was added to rims on pitchers, basins, bowls, etc. more as a protective measure than a decorative one.

As enameling processes were perfected, colors used abroad were often inspired by the vibrant hues found in the beauty of the countryside or the colors that predominated during any given stylistic period. In addition, the much celebrated Art Nouveau era of the late 1800s and early twentieth century turned greater attention towards the glory and beauty of mother nature. For example, an early 1900s catalog released by the German manufacturing company, Annweiler, noted their enameled ware was produced in colors such as red copper, cloudy gray, dark blue, white, terra cotta, and iris—colors inspired no doubt by the beauty of the sky, the richness of the earth, and the glory of a floral bouquet.

As color became a more significant aspect in household and kitchen decoration, new shades were developed and proved quite popular. During the 1930s Léopold and Company of France was turning out enameled ware in appealing

European canister set, ribbed, with matching salt box and match box. Red with floral graphic design. *Courtesy of Pamela DeBisschop.*

shades of color and color combinations such as turquoise, marbled light green and coral, marbled blue and maroon, fire-cured orange, speckled chestnut, cloudy blue, and terra cotta. At the same time, another German shop, that of Bing Werke, was offering their enameled ware goods in white, green, pink, blue, granite, yellow, olive green, brown, and chocolate-maroon.

European coffee pot, 10" tall, "end of the day" coloring with green, pink, and white. *Courtesy of David T. Pikul, The Chuctanunda Antique Co.* $300-400.

Early on, color was used more extensively in enameled production in Europe but American manufacturers soon made up for lost time. Initially many American firms produced large quantities of enameled ware in a solid gray color or a mottled gray that could be achieved with a singular coating of enamel. Many believe this to be the origin of the generic term "granite ware" in the United States for some of the early gray pieces did have an almost granite-like appearance. Others believe that the name suggested the durability of the rock, granite.

Regardless of the fact that colored enameled ware required anywhere from two to four enamel coatings to achieve the desired shade and effect (resulting in an increase in cost production), it was the wave of the future. By the early 1920s the American kitchen, long ignored from a decorating standpoint, suddenly became the center of intense focus. Not only did manufacturers, architects, and household or domestic science experts explore the concept of greater convenience in the kitchen, but they also sought ways to make it more cheerful. Enameled ware manufacturers stepped up their production and introduction of colored goods and before the end of the decade record amounts of enameled ware were being produced in red, green, blue, yellow, violet, brown, and numerous variations of these and other colors. Department stores furthered the cause and during the late 1920s Macy's and others participated in a "Color in the Kitchen" campaign that spotlighted the extensive variety of colorful kitchenware items available. Enameled ware manufacturers and others turned out goods in so many colors in fact, that "standardization" became a new watchword among those in the housewares industry.

Color as it related to the kitchen was so important that by 1937 a Color Standardization Committee was formed under the auspices of the U.S. Department of Commerce to adopt

European salt box, ribbed, pink, with French lettering done in gold. *Courtesy of David T. Pikul, The Chuctanunda Antique Co.* $175-225.

industry-wide standards in regard to color for kitchen accessories. The final outcome included white, kitchen green, ivory, Delphinium blue, Royal blue, and red. Fortunately for collectors, this standardization came a little too late for the enameled ware industry which had been producing many more colors than those listed above and had actually seen their best years pass as stiff competition from glass and aluminum goods began to effect their market.

For enameled ware manufacturers in the United States their achievement of certain colors was often as much a secret as their production techniques. They took enormous pride in their line of colors and gave them prominent names. For example, Lalance and Grosjean turned out a line called "Flint Grey," the Strong Manufacturing Company offered colored enameled ware marketed as "Alice Blue," "Ripe Concord Grape," and "Emerald Ware," the United States Stamping Company had "U.S. Ivory" and "U.S. Bisque," and Norvel Shapleigh distributed a decorative line called "Bluebelle Ware." Other American firms were also noted for their lines of colored goods such as the Canton Stamping and Enameling Company which produced ivory items with green trim (popular during the late 1920s and the 1930s) and various pastel shades. The Columbian Enameling and Stamping Company manufactured a line called "Onyx" with a brown and white mottled finish, and the Lisk Manufacturing Company made enameled ware available in attractive shades such as robin's-egg blue, cobalt blue, and dark green.

Color, then, as it pertains to vintage enameled ware, was born of the beauty of the French and European countryside and propelled to department store shelves by the ongoing quest for "modern" amenities in the circa 1920s American home. The vision of the artisan and the vision of the manufacturer coincided in time. The end result was everyday objects as lovely and cheerful as they were functional.

European canister set, blue with white checks, red trim, and French lettering. *Courtesy of David T. Pikul, The Chuctanunda Antique Co.* $400-500.

European lavabo, "end of the day" color pattern with brown, white, and green. *Courtesy of Stephen Smith, Foundation Antiques.* $300-500.

Large European coffee biggin, 14" tall, double handles. White with blue shading and decorative graphic design. *Courtesy of David T. Pikul, The Chuctanunda Antique Co.* $400-500.

American milk pail (10" tall) and cream pail (8" tall), gray mottled with metal lids and handles. *Courtesy of Tom & Lorraine Zavorskas, Cobweb Corner Antiques.* $150-200 each.

European utensil rack with tools, light brown with dark brown trim and graphic design. *Courtesy of David T. Pikul, The Chuctanunda Antique Co.* $175-225.

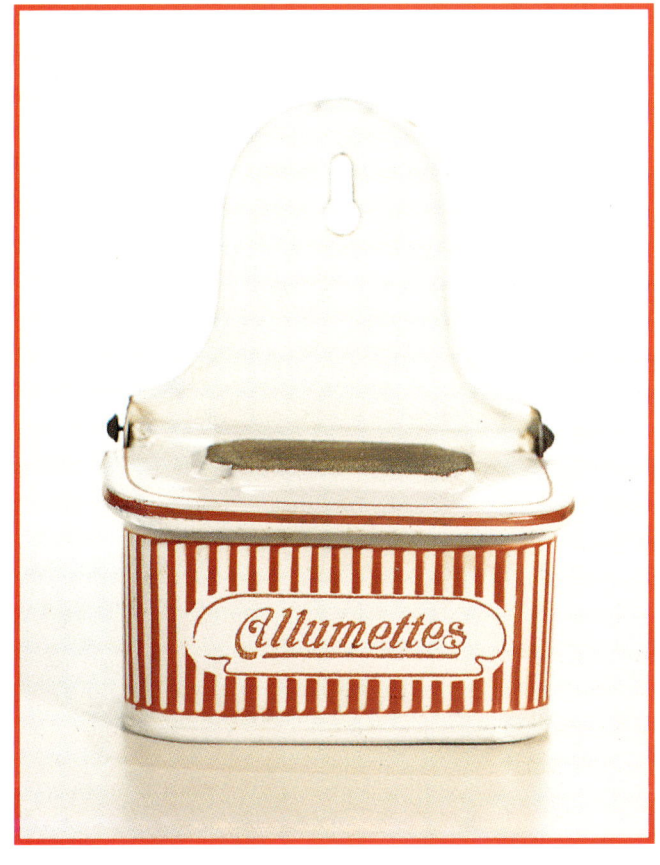

European measuring pitcher, 7" tall, green with lily pad floral design. *Courtesy of David T. Pikul, The Chuctanunda Antique Co.* $150-200.

European match box, white with red stripes and French lettering. *Courtesy of David T. Pikul, The Chuctanunda Antique Co.* $150-200.

American coffee pot, 10" tall, white with metal lid and wooden handle. *Courtesy of Tom & Lorraine Zavorskas, Cobweb Corner Antiques.* $150-200.

*Right:* American chamber pail, 11" tall, green shaded "Shamrock Ware" with wire/wooden handle. *Courtesy of Tom & Lorraine Zavorskas, Cobweb Corner Antiques.* $200-275.

European teapot, 5" tall, yellow and red shaded, marked "Yugoslavia." *Courtesy of Betty Duquet.* $75-100.

*Above:* European body pitcher, 15" tall, ribbed, robin's egg blue with gilt trim. *Courtesy of Ellen M. Plante.* $200-250.

*Right:* European salt box, ribbed, orange with white banding and French lettering. *Courtesy of David T. Pikul, The Chuctanunda Antique Co.* $150-200.

European canister set, red with blue graphic design and French lettering. *Courtesy of David T. Pikul, The Chuctanunda Antique Co.* $500-600.

European coffee biggin, 12" tall, exceptional blue with floral graphics and red trim. *Courtesy of David T. Pikul, The Chuctanunda Antique Co.* $400-500.

*Opposite page:*
European utensil rack, cream with blue diamond design. *Courtesy of David T. Pikul, The Chuctanunda Antique Co.* $175-225.

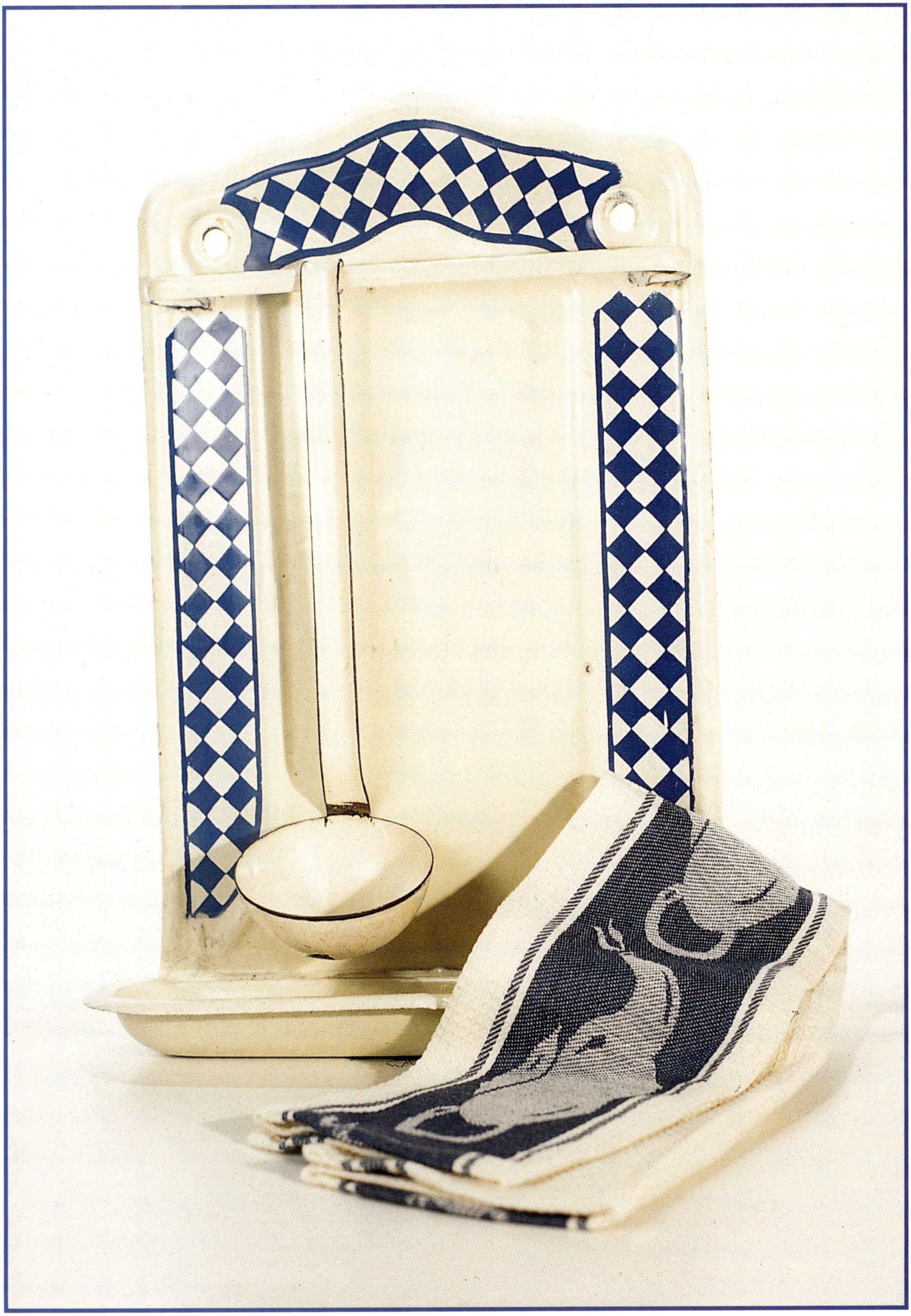

European lavabo, white with blue floral design. *Courtesy of David T. Pikul, The Chuctanunda Antique Co.* $350-500.

European measuring pitcher, 10" tall, "end of the day" coloring with green, white, and brown. *Courtesy of Stephen Smith, Foundation Antiques.* $225-275.

American coffee pot, 8" tall, brown and white mottled with metal lid and wooden handle. *Courtesy of Tom & Lorraine Zavorskas, Cobweb Corner Antiques.* $225-300.

European coffee pot, 9" tall, rare blue and white droopy check with red trim. *Courtesy of Stephen Smith, Foundation Antiques.* $400-475.

European enamel over cast-iron jug, 10" tall, multi-colored, extremely rare item and coloring. *Courtesy of Stephen Smith, Foundation Antiques.* $600-800.

European trivet, 8" size, cobalt blue with white checkered design. *Courtesy of David T. Pikul, The Chuctanunda Antique Co.* $125-150.

European irrigator, 9" tall, brown and white relish pattern. *Courtesy of Stephen Smith, Foundation Antiques.* $130-165.

European flask, 6" tall, gray mottled. *Courtesy of Stephen Smith, Foundation Antiques.* $125-175.

American cream carrier, 8" tall, light blue. *Courtesy of Betty Duquet.* $95-125.

European salt box, orange relish pattern with French lettering. *Courtesy of David T. Pikul, The Chuctanunda Antique Co.* $150-200.

American teapot, 6" tall, gray mottled with ornate metal trim. *Courtesy of Stephen Smith, Foundation Antiques.* $200-300.

European lidded pot, 5" tall, enamel over cast-iron, unusual blue and white pattern. *Courtesy of Stephen Smith, Foundation Antiques.* $125-175.

European coffee server with spigot, 22" tall, green and white mottled. *Courtesy of Stephen Smith, Foundation Antiques.* $600-750.

European canister set, ribbed, brick red with green shading and French lettering. *Courtesy of Stephen Smith, Foundation Antiques.* $300-400.

65

European enamel over cast-iron vase, 8" tall, gray coloring. *Courtesy of Stephen Smith, Foundation Antiques.* $50-75.

European coffee biggin, 10" tall, blue and white shading to create large checkered design. *Courtesy of David T. Pikul, The Chuctanunda Antique Co.* $225-300.

American roaster, 15" size, red with black handles, embossed with "Savory." *Courtesy of Betty Duquet.* $100-150.

European colander, 12" size, white with blue checkered design. *Courtesy of Stephen Smith, Foundation Antiques.* $85-125.

European double boiler, 8" tall, gray mottled. *Courtesy of Stephen Smith, Foundation Antiques.* $225-250.

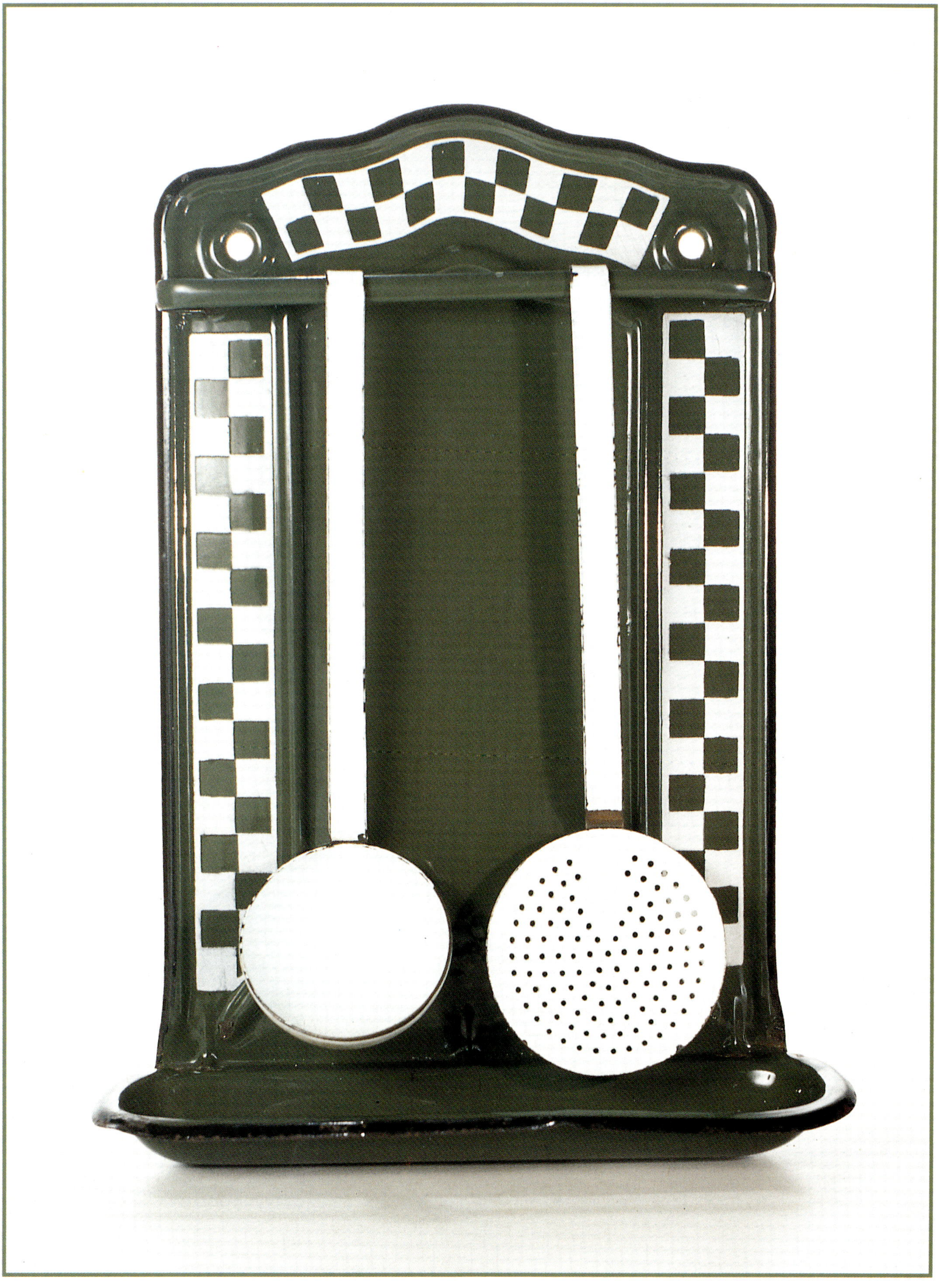

European trivet, 9 1/2" size, pink shading. *Courtesy of Stephen Smith, Foundation Antiques.* $125-175.

Large European coffee biggin, 12" tall, double handles, "end of the day" coloring with red, brown, and purple. *Courtesy of Stephen Smith, Foundation Antiques.* $300-400.

American canteen, 6" tall, gray mottled with metal cap. *Courtesy of Stephen Smith, Foundation Antiques.* $200-225.

*Opposite page:*
European utensil rack with tools, green with checkered design. *Courtesy of David T. Pikul, The Chuctanunda Antique Co.* $200-250.

Large European coffee biggin, 14" tall, double handles, white with yellow shading, blue trim, and floral graphic design. *Courtesy of Pamela DeBisschop.* $400-500.

*Above:* American covered kettle, 6" tall, aqua and white swirl with black trim, circa 1930s. *Courtesy of Betty Duquet.* $100-150.

*Below:* European (Scandanavian) wall-hung laundry set, 6" tall containers for scouring powder, soda, and soap. Red with white lettering. *Courtesy of Susan Curran, Snow Leopard Antiques.* $60-75 each.

*Right:* European (Austrian) syrup pitcher, 6" tall, medium blue, marked "B. Fres." *Courtesy of Betty Duquet.* $75-100.

European utensil rack with tools, multi-color stripe design with red, white, purple, and blue. *Courtesy of Pamela DeBisschop.* $200-300.

European coffee pot, 9" tall, rare pink with floral graphic design. *Courtesy of Susan Curran, Snow Leopard Antiques.* $300-400.

European coffee pot, 8 1/2" tall, light blue with darker blue and white graphic design. *Courtesy of David T. Pikul, The Chuctanunda Antique Co.* $150-200.

European milk pail, 11" tall, red with wire/wooden handle. *Courtesy of Betty Duquet.* $75-125.

American tea kettle, 6" tall, gray mottled. *Courtesy of Stan & MaryAnn Szambelan.* $150-175.

European match box and salt box, rare orange and blue coloring, French lettering. *Courtesy of Susan Curran, Snow Leopard Antiques.* Match box $200-275 and salt box $250-300.

European canister set, ribbed, yellow with black shading and French script. *Courtesy of David T. Pikul, The Chuctanunda Antique Co.* $350-400.

European coffee pot, 9 1/2" tall, orange and white shaded with floral graphic design. *Courtesy of David T. Pikul, The Chuctanunda Antique Co.* $275-350.

American covered kettle, 6 1/2" tall, dark green and white mottled (Chrysolite). *Courtesy of Betty Duquet.* $200-250.

European canister set, rare coloring, white with black and yellow check design, French lettering. *Courtesy of David T. Pikul, The Chuctanunda Antique Co.* $400-500.

English canisters, ribbed, pale blue with white lettering. *Courtesy of Susan Curran, Snow Leopard Antiques.* $60-75 each.

European coffee pot, 8" tall, hinged lid, brown. *Courtesy of David T. Pikul, The Chuctanunda Antique Co.* $175-250.

European (Scandanavian) utility set with wall-hung containers for scouring powder, bar soap, and brushes. Yellow with black lettering. *Courtesy of Susan Curran, Snow Leopard Antiques.* $95-125 each.

European utensil rack with matching utensils, pale blue. *Courtesy of Betty Duquet.* $175-225.

European coffee pot, 9" tall, red with floral graphic design. *Courtesy of Susan Curran, Snow Leopard Antiques.* $200-300.

European coffee biggin, 9" tall, white with pale blue stripes and decorative garland of roses. *Courtesy of Pamela DeBisschop.*

American mug, 4 1/2" tall, cobalt blue and white mottled. *Courtesy Betty Duquet.* $225-275.

European match box, yellow with decorative red trim and French lettering. *Courtesy of David T. Pikul, The Cuctanunda Antique Co.* $150-200.

European canister set, extremely rare color combination of yellow and blue shading with red Art Deco graphic design and French lettering. *Courtesy of David T. Pikul, The Chuctanunda Antique Co.* $600-700.

European covered kettle, 6" tall, green and white mottled. *Courtesy of Stephen Smith, Foundation Antiques.* $200-250.

American coffee pot, 8" tall, light brown and white relish pattern, metal lid, wooden handle. *Courtesy of Betty Duquet.* $200-300.

European soap/sponge/toothbrush holder, one red, one yellow. *Courtesy of Susan Curran, Snow Leopard Antiques.* $95-125 each.

European syrup pitcher (4" tall) and trivet (8" size) in medium blue. *Courtesy of Betty Duquet.* Pitcher $45-65 and trivet $50-75.

European vase, 8" tall gray. *Courtesy of Stephen Smith, Foundation Antiques.* $50-75.

American water pitcher, 10" tall, blue and white swirl with black trim. *Courtesy of Betty Duquet.* $250-300.

Large European coffee biggin, double handles, blue with floral graphic design. *Courtesy of Susan Curran, Snow Leopard Antiques.* $500-600.

European measuring pitcher, 8" tall, red and white mottled. *Courtesy of Stan & MaryAnn Szambelan.* $175-225.

European coffee biggin, 12" tall, light blue with black trim. *Courtesy of Betty Duquet.* $125-150.

European candlesticks, light blue and red. *Courtesy of Betty Duquet.* $35-50 each.

European (Polish) milk pail, 9 1/2" tall, yellow with wire/wooden handle. Marked "S" inside a V-shaped logo. *Courtesy of Betty Duquet.* $50-75.

European canister set, five pieces, red with floral graphic design. *Courtesy of Pam DeBisschop.* $400-500.

European canister set, rare yellow with black and white checkered design and French script. *Courtesy of Pamela DeBisschop.* $500-600.

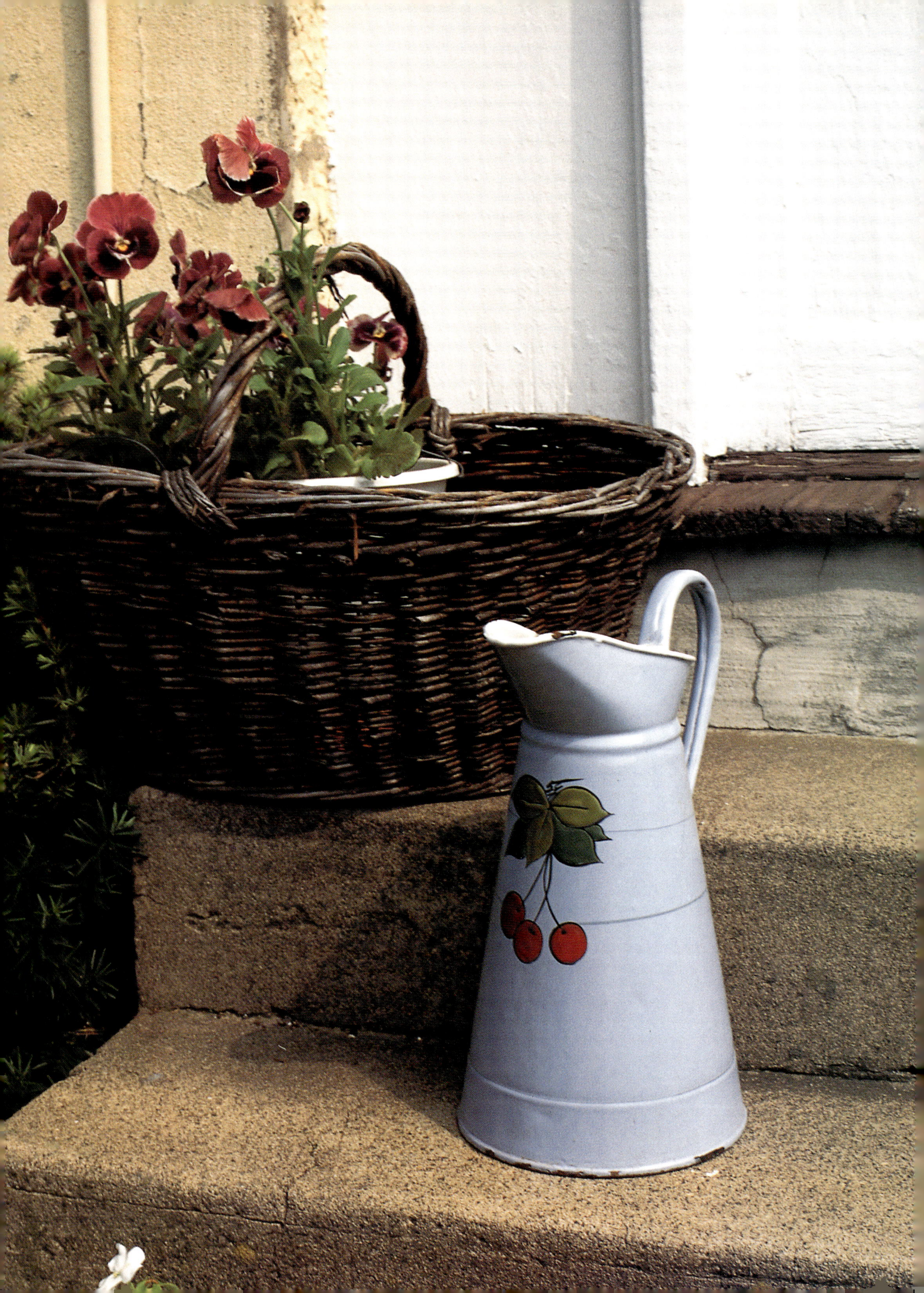

American coffee pot, 9" tall, gray mottled with label for "Purity Enameled Ware." *Courtesy of David T. Pikul, The Chuctanunda Antique Co.* $125-175.

American oval butter kettle/carrier, 7 1/4" tall, aqua and white swirl with black trim. *Courtesy of David T. Pikul, The Chuctanunda Antique Co.* $275-325.

*Right:* American teapot, 5" tall, cream colored with green trim. *Courtesy of David T. Pikul, The Chuctanunda Antique Co.* $50-75.

*Opposite page:*
European body pitcher, 14 1/2" tall, light blue with fruit (cherry) motif. *Courtesy of Pamela DeBisschop.* $250-300.

European kitchenware items, white with red trim, includes 7" tall milk pail, 5" tall lidded pitcher, and assorted pans. *Courtesy of David T. Pikul, The Chuctanunda Antique Co.* Milk pail $75-125, pitcher $100-150, and pots $150-225.

European teapot, 4 1/2" tall, orange with black trim and black and white checkered design. *Courtesy of David T. Pikul, The Chuctanunda Antique Co.* $250-300.

88

European canister set, cream with green trim and French lettering. *Courtesy of David T. Pikul, The Chuctanunda Antique Co.* $400-500.

European coffee biggin, 9 1/2" tall, cream with dark green trim. *Courtesy of David T. Pikul, The Chuctanunda Antique Co.* $75-125.

American teapot, 6" tall, robin's egg blue and white mottled with ornate metal trim. *Courtesy of Betty Duquet.* $250-275.

European teapot, 8" tall, red with red, white, and black feather pattern. *Courtesy of David T. Pikul, The Chuctanunda Antique Co.* $200-300.

European pans, assorted sizes, "French blue" color with blue and white check design. *Courtesy of David T. Pikul, The Chuctanunda Antique Co.* $175-225.

European coffee biggin, 9 1/2" tall, rare yellow color with black creating a check design. *Courtesy of David T. Pikul, The Chuctanunda Antique Co.* $300-400.

# Chapter Three
# Decorative Enameled Ware Styles

The enameled ware produced for household use during the late 1800s through the 1930s was often turned out in a variety of decorative styles that made the everyday items a cheerful addition to kitchens and households in general, both here in the United States and abroad. Patterns included broad swirled, marbled, mottled, relished, spattered, feathered, and shaded along with those known as confetti, chickenwire, and "snow on the mountain."

While each individual manufacturer had their own production methods for achieving the desired results, decorative patterns or styles were generally created by air brushing, hand-dipping an item in a secondary enameled ware color, machine dipping, or instrument (tong) dipping.

Each process involved a high level of skill and production workers became specialists in turning out pieces with the various decorative effects. One exception to these assorted processes was the manner in which the mottled or marbled design was first achieved on the earliest examples of gray enameled ware produced in the United States. Known as selective etching, this was a process whereby the manner of drying achieved a marbleized pattern. This could be done with a singular coating of enamel and the degree of acids in the mix caused the base metal to rust and develop the decorative marbleized appearance.

A very different method was used to create bi-colored pieces with a marbleized pattern. The item was dipped in a base color (often white), and then dipped a second time in a different color. During firing, the white base coat passed through or blended with the second color resulting in a marbleized finish. This was often practiced by European manufacturers. Yet another method involved the use of enamel slips and soda crystals that caused a marbled effect when the item was placed in the kiln for firing

Decorative effects such as the spattered or speckled patterns found on vintage enameled ware were early on achieved simply enough; the style was created by hand spattering flecks of color or using a brush to do the same. As enameled ware

*Opposite page:*
European body pitcher, beautiful red and white swirl. *Courtesy of Pamela DeBisschop.*

European canister set, blue and white marbled with French lettering. *Courtesy of Betty Duquet.* $295-365.

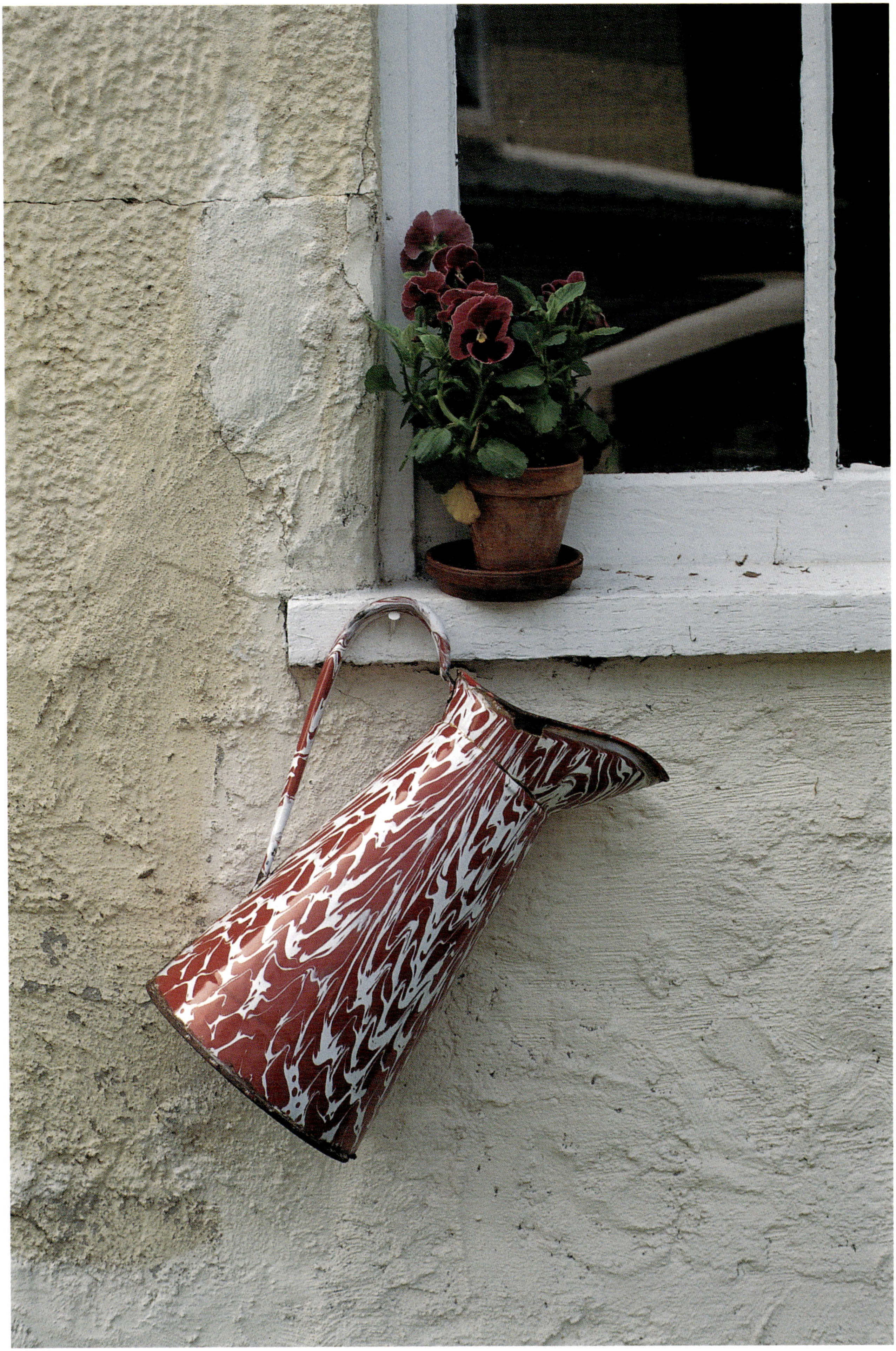

production became more mechanized, a contrasting color was added to the molten glass or frit that served as the basic formula for making enamel.

Shaded enameled ware was produced by a spray gun that applied lighter or darker shades of color as the piece rotated on a mechanical surface. Swirl designs were often the result of the level of skill possessed by factory workers who would dip a piece and allow the enamel to run in such a way that a style or pattern was created. The decorative style known as "Snow on the Mountain," because it does indeed resemble white snow on a mound, was accomplished by applying thick coats of white enamel over the top of a colored base coat. Because the white was applied so heavily, the finished product had a bumpy, snowy look, with traces of the base coat showing through.

"End of the day" is the name collectors have given to enameled ware sporting three or more colors in the decorative design. The name is fitting because in all likelihood such pieces resulted from workers simply using up the various color glazes at the end of the work day, although "end of the day" pieces may have been the purposeful result of whimsical and creative dipping. "End of the day" items were turned out both here and abroad but while many European examples have a chicken wire pattern, pieces made in the States often resulted in a marbleized effect.

And what about the plain, solid color enameled ware with a decorative trim? Actually, many pieces produced early on were a singular shade and devoid of pattern. During the late 1800s and early 1900s white was favored throughout Europe with a black or dark blue trim. In the United States like

European pans, "end of the day" swirl pattern with red, blue, and white. *Courtesy of David T. Pikul, The Chuctanunda Antique Co.* $275-325.

colors were used as well as red for beading. By the 1920s and 1930s cream with green trim was especially popular in the United States. In England, where solid colors were highly favored, pale blue, yellow, cream, and white pieces were decorated and protected with black, blue, or green trim.

The decorative styles featured on enameled ware are evidence of the artisan's skill. And as many of the enamel "recipes" and techniques still remain secret long after shops and factories have closed, one could consider it a lost art form. With this in mind, a growing number of collectors have realized the almost folk-art quality, or potential for same, in beautiful, vintage enameled ware.

European coffee pot, 9" tall, pink, white, and green "end of the day" marbled pattern. *Courtesy of David T. Pikul, The Chuctanunda Antique Co.* $275-325.

American potato kettle, 7" tall, blue and white marbled. *Courtesy of David T. Pikul, The Chuctanunda Antique Co.* $275-350.

American milk carrier, 11" tall, light blue and white speckle with dark blue lid and wire handle. *Courtesy of Betty Duquet.* $125-150.

European utensil rack, 20" length, orange and white mottled. *Courtesy of David T. Pikul, The Chuctanunda Antique Co.* $200-275.

European coffee biggin, 10 1/2" tall, blue and white chicken wire pattern with red trim. *Courtesy of David T. Pikul, The Chuctanunda Antique Co.* $325-400.

American saucepan, 8" size, blue and white swirl with black handle. *Courtesy of Betty Duquet.* $175-225.

American water pitcher, 5 1/2" tall, rare "end of the day" coloring with red, blue, white, and green swirl. *Courtesy of Stan & MaryAnn Szambelan.* $400-500.

European jug, 7 1/2" tall, blue and white chicken wire pattern. *Courtesy of Stephen Smith, Foundation Antiques.* $325-375.

American kettle, 5" tall, cobalt blue and white swirl. *Courtesy of Betty Duquet.* $250-275.

American measuring pitcher, 8" tall, gray mottled. *Courtesy of Tom & Lorraine Zavorskas, Cobweb Corner Antiques.* $150-175.

European coffee biggin, 10 1/2" tall, rare red and white mottled. *Courtesy of David T. Pikul, The Chuctanunda Antique Co.* $350-500.

American coffee pot, 12" tall, medium blue and white mottled. *Courtesy of Betty Duquet.* $150-175.

American milk carrier, 10 1/2" tall, rare brown and white swirl. *Courtesy of Tom & Lorraine Zavorskas, Cobweb Corner Antiques.* $400-500.

European salt box, rare green and white mottled with French script. *Courtesy of David T. Pikul, The Chuctanunda Antique Co.* $200-250.

European match box, orange and white feather pattern with black trim. *Courtesy of Susan Curran, Snow Leopard Antiques.* $175-225.

American covered pail, 6 1/2" tall, blue shaded pattern. *Courtesy of Betty Duquet.* $150-175.

European canister set, yellow and white mottled. *Courtesy of David T. Pikul, The Chuctanunda Antique Co.* $400-500.

European coffee biggin, 10 1/2" tall, blue and white swirl with black trim. *Courtesy of David T. Pikul, The Chuctanunda Antique Co.* $350-500.

European candlestick, rare "end of the day" coloring with green, white, and brown marbled pattern, blue trim. *Courtesy of Stephen Smith, Foundation Antiques.* $225-300.

American coffee biggin (these were often advertised simply as French "coffee pots") 10" tall, light blue and white mottled with ornate metal trim. Marked "Manning Bowman." *Courtesy of Betty Duquet.* $375-425.

American milk pail, 10" tall, gray mottled, marked "Granite Iron Ware." *Courtesy of Betty Duquet.* $175-225.

American coffee boiler, 13" tall, green shaded "Shamrock Ware." *Courtesy of Tom & Lorraine Zavorskas, Cobweb Corner Antiques.* $300-375.

American coffee pot (8 1/2" tall) and matching saucepans, red and white swirl, circa 1930s. *Courtesy of Betty Duquet.* Coffee pot $200-275; saucepans $75-95 each.

American kettle, 6 1/2" tall, blue and white swirl with black handles. *Courtesy of David T. Pikul, The Chuctanunda Antique Co.* $150-200.

American coffee pot, 11" tall, blue and white relish pattern, metal lid and wooden handle. *Courtesy of Betty Duquet.* $200-250.

European teapot, 5 3/4" tall, solid blue with black trim, marked "Poland." *Courtesy of Betty Duquet.* $40-75.

American tea kettle, 7" tall, aqua and white swirl, circa 1930s. *Courtesy of Betty Duquet.* $175-200.

American water pitcher, 9" tall, solid orange with black trim and white interior. *Courtesy of Betty Duquet.* $50-75.

American measuring pitcher, 9 1/2" tall, black with white speckles. Marked "USN." *Courtesy of Betty Duquet.* $50-75.

American tea kettle, 10" tall, cobalt blue and white marbled, wire and wooden handle. *Courtesy of Tom & Lorainne Zavorskas, Cobweb Corner Antiques.* $375-425.

European teapot, 5" tall, multi-colored feather pattern. *Courtesy of David T. Pikul, The Chuctanunda Antique Co.* $225-275.

American chamber pot, 4" tall, cobalt blue and white swirl. *Courtesy of David T. Pikul, The Chuctanunda Antique Co.* $175-250.

American berry bucket, 3 3/4" tall, light blue and white swirl. *Courtesy of David T. Pikul, The Chuctanunda Antique Co.* $175-225.

American tea kettle, 7" tall, yellow and white swirl, circa 1930s. *Courtesy of Tom & Lorraine Zavorskas, Cobweb Corner Antiques.* $150-200.

American coffee pot, 9 1/2" tall, unusual blue and white wavy mottled pattern. *Courtesy of David T. Pikul, The Chuctanunda Antique Co.* $325-400.

European canister set, ribbed, blue and white shading with French lettering and gilt trim. *Courtesy of David T. Pikul, The Chuctanunda Antique Co.* $300-400.

Opposite page:
European lavabo hung on a wooden board commonly used for this purpose. "End of the day" coloring with green, white, and brown marbled. *Courtesy of Pamela DeBisschop.*

American milk pail, 9 3/4" tall, blue and white swirl with double metal handles. *Courtesy of David T. Pikul, The Chuctanunda Antique Co.* $300-400.

European wall-hung flour box, blue and white chicken wire pattern with German lettering. *Courtesy of Susan Curran, Snow Leopard Antiques.* $275-325.

European teapot, 6" tall, rare multi-colored feather pattern with red trim. *Courtesy of Susan Curran, Snow Leopard Antiques.* $250-325.

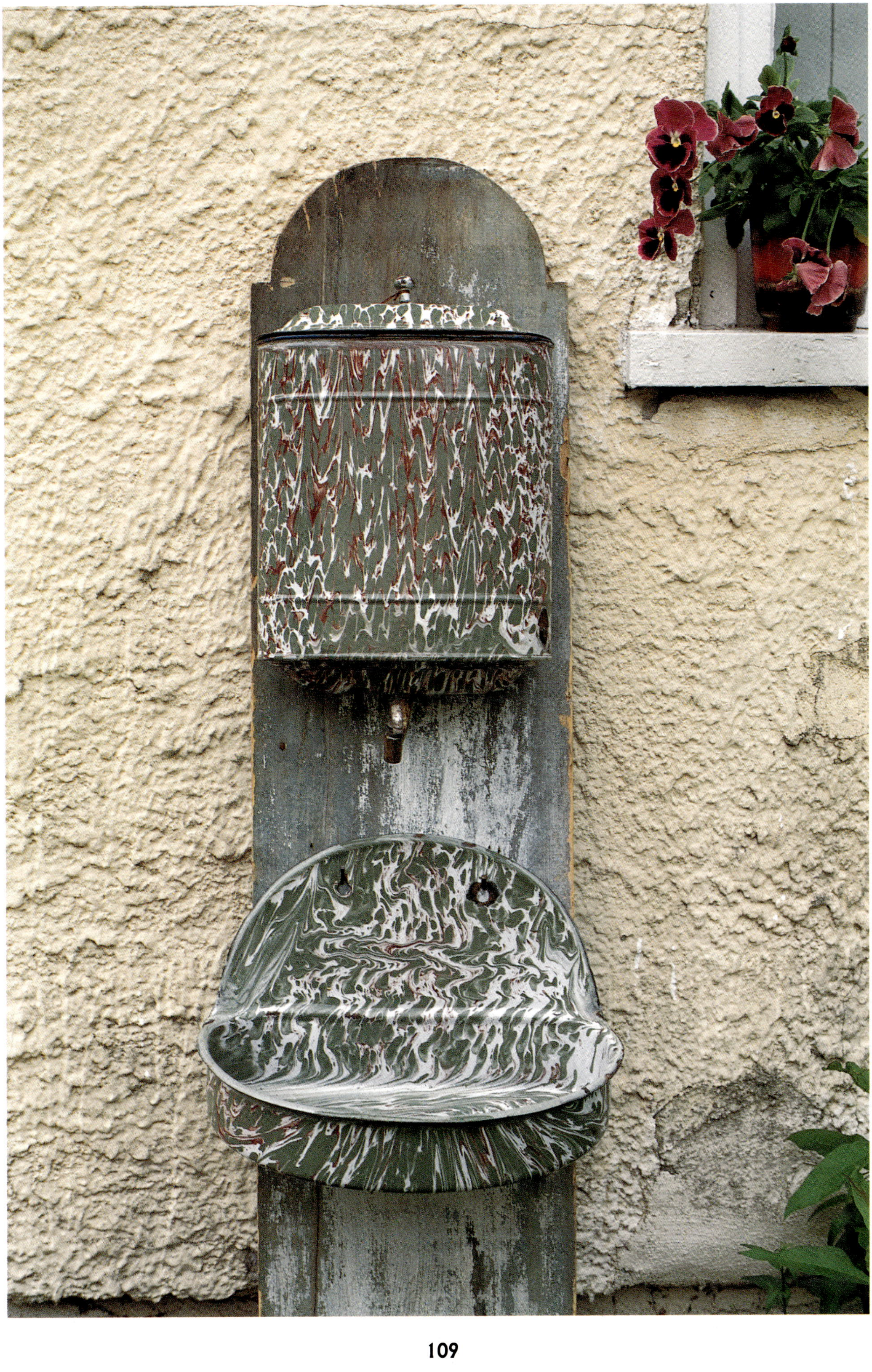

American lidded pail, 5 3/4" tall, cobalt blue and white relish pattern. *Courtesy of David T. Pikul, The Chuctanunda Antique Co.* $175-225.

European body pitcher, 15" tall, yellow and white swirl with black trim. *Courtesy of Susan Curran, Snow Leopard Antiques.* $375-450.

European wall-hung three-cup laundry set, rare orange and blue mottled, French lettering for sand, soap, and soda. *Courtesy of Susan Curran, Snow Leopard Antiques.* $275-350.

American candlestick, 6" size, rare cobalt blue and white swirl with scalloped edge. *Courtesy of David T. Pikul, The Chuctanunda Antique Co.* $300-400.

American potato kettle, 6 1/2" tall, blue and white mottled with wire and wooden handle. *Courtesy of David T. Pikul, The Chuctanunda Antique Co.* $275-350.

European sugar and creamer (5 1/2" tall), rare "end of the day" relish pattern. *Courtesy of Susan Curran, Snow Leopard Antiques.* $275-350 each piece.

American saucepan, 3 3/4" tall, cobalt blue and white swirl (redipped over light blue). *Courtesy of David T. Pikul, The Chuctanunda Antique Co.* $225-300.

European (French) coffee biggin, 10" tall, blue and white feather pattern, original decal. *Courtesy of David T. Pikul, The Chuctanunda Antique Co.* $200-275.

European lidded carrier, 11" tall, red and white mottled. *Courtesy of David T. Pikul, The Chuctanunda Antique Co.* $275-325.

American miner's dinner bucket, 7 1/4" tall, blue and white swirl. *Courtesy of David T. Pikul, The Chuctanunda Antique Co.* $300-400.

European canisters (partial set), "end of the day" relish pattern with red trim and French lettering. *Courtesy of Susan Curran, Snow Leopard Antiques.* $250-325.

European body pitcher, 14 1/2" tall, red and white feather pattern with gilt trim. *Courtesy of Susan Curran, Snow Leopard Antiques.* $175-300.

American water pitcher, 7 1/2" tall, cobalt blue and white swirl. *Courtesy of David T. Pikul, The Chuctanunda Antique Co.* $200-300.

American coffee boiler, 11" tall, rare brown and white swirl with metal lid. *Courtesy of Tom & Lorraine Zavorskas, Cobweb Antiques.* $400-500.

European coffee biggin, 9 1/2" tall, cobalt blue and white marbled. *Courtesy of David T. Pikul, The Chuctanunda Antique Co.* $300-400.

European wall-hung salt box, red and white marbled with French lettering. *Courtesy of Susan Curran, Snow Leopard Antiques.* $175-250.

American convex kettle, 7" tall, blue and white swirl. *Courtesy of Betty Duquet.* $225-275.

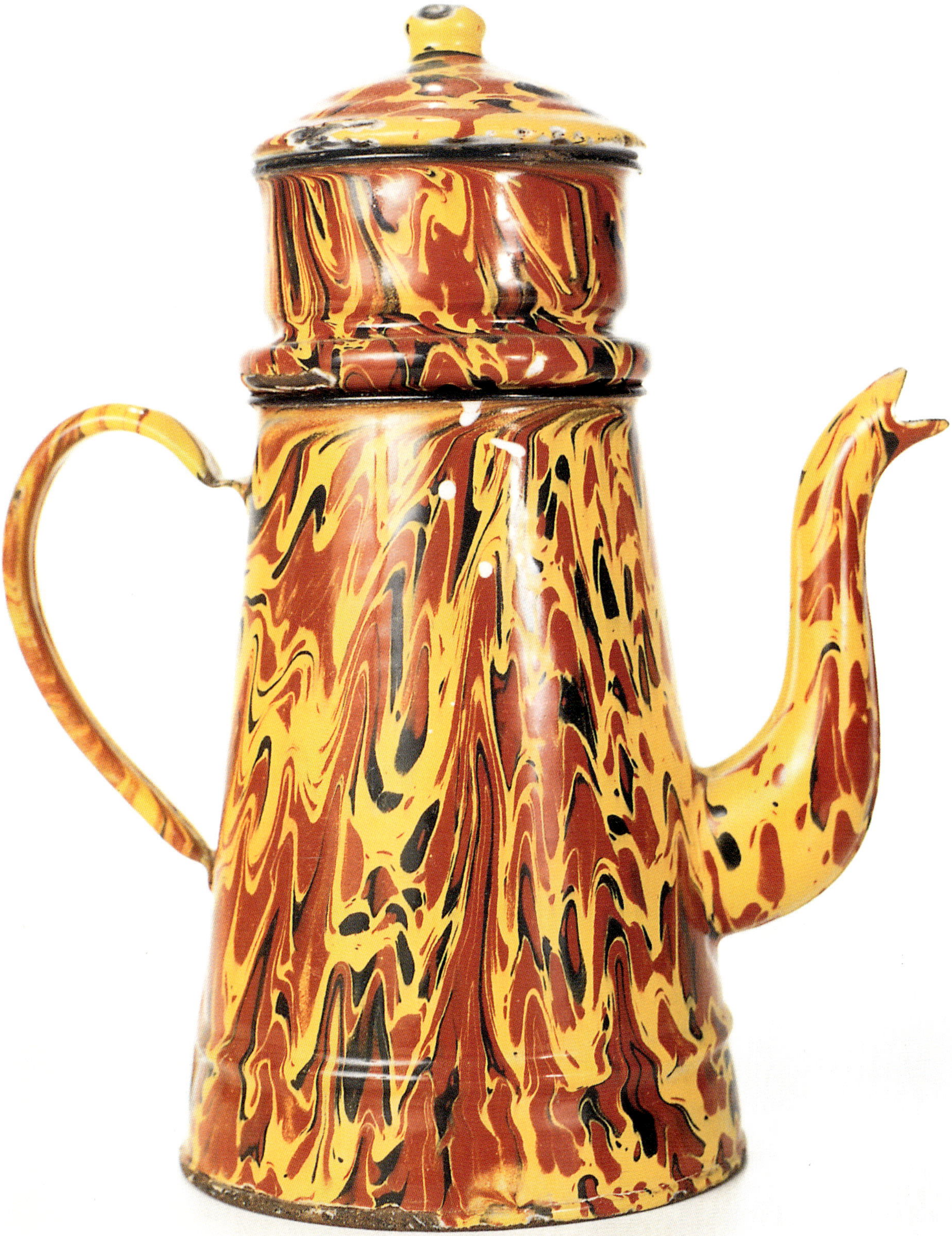

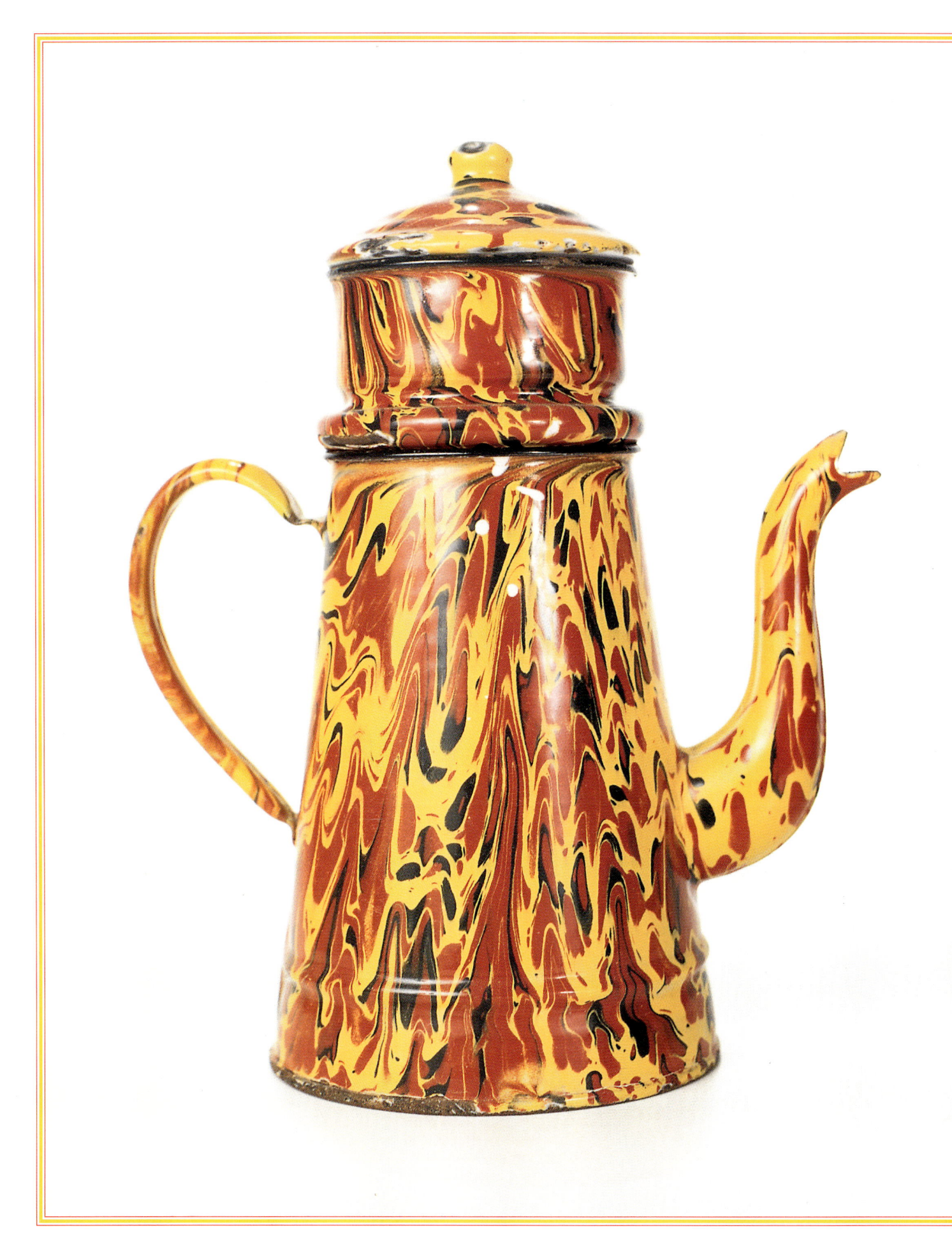

European wall-hung towel rack, white and orange mottled with French lettering in red. *Courtesy of Susan Curran, Snow Leopard Antiques.* $150-175.

American Berlin kettle, 3 1/2" tall, blue and white swirl. *Courtesy of David T. Pikul, The Chuctanunda Antique Co.* $175-250.

Opposite page:
European coffee biggin, 9 1/2" tall, rare "end of the day" swirl pattern. *Courtesy of Susan Curran, Snow Leopard Antiques.* $650-800.

European salt box, red and white mottled, French lettering. *Courtesy of Susan Curran, Snow Leopard Antiques.* $200-275.

European match box, rare red and white feather pattern. *Courtesy of Susan Curran, Snow Leopard Antiques.* $200-300.

American coffee boiler, 14" tall, blue and white marbled. *Courtesy of David T. Pikul, The Chuctanunda Antique Co.* $225-275.

European wall-hung potholder basket, blue and white chicken wire pattern with German lettering. *Courtesy of Susan Curran, Snow Leopard Antiques.* $300-375.

American milk pail, 9" tall, rare cobalt blue and white swirl. *Courtesy of David T. Pikul, The Chuctanunda Antique Co.* $500-600.

European candlestick, 6" size, scalloped, rare gray and white swirl pattern. *Courtesy of Stan & MaryAnn Szambelan.* $200-225.

European rice ball, 4" size, rare item, blue and white mottled. *Courtesy of David T. Pikul, The Chuctanunda Antique Co.* $175-250.

European coffee biggin, 9 1/2" tall, red and white marbled with red trim. *Courtesy of David T. Pikul, The Chuctanunda Antique Co.* $225-300.

European coffee pot, 9" tall, green and white mottled. *Courtesy of David T. Pikul, The Chuctanunda Antique Co.* $200-250.

European canister set, red and white mottled with red trim and French lettering. Note the canister marked "PATES," which translates into pasta. *Courtesy of Susan Curran, Snow Leopard Antiques.* $300-400.

European utensil rack, rare blue and white wavy mottling. *Courtesy of Susan Curran, Snow Leopard Antiques.* $375-450.

European body pitcher, 14" tall, "end of the day" pink, white, and blue swirl with black trim. *Courtesy of David T. Pikul, The Chuctanunda Antique Co.* $350-400.

European wall-hung laundry set, red and white mottled with French lettering. *Courtesy of David T. Pikul, The Chuctanunda Antique Co.* $275-325.

121

European coffee pot, 9" tall, rare "end of the day" red, white, and blue in a chicken wire pattern. *Courtesy of Stan & MaryAnn Szambelan.* $600-700.

*Bottom left:* European salt box, rounded shape with wooden lid, blue and white marbled, French lettering. *Courtesy of David T. Pikul, The Chuctanunda Antique Co.* $150-200.

*Bottom right:* American teapot, 7" tall, gray mottled with metal hinged lid. *Courtesy of David T. Pikul, The Chuctanunda Antique Co.* $175-225.

American cuspidor, 5" tall, blue and white mottled. Labeled "Lisk." See next photo. *Courtesy of Stan & MaryAnn Szambelan.* $225-300.

Previous item (cuspidor) with "Lisk" label.

European irrigator, 10" tall, blue and white swirl. *Courtesy of David T. Pikul, The Chuctanunda Antique Co.* $225-275.

European footed colander, 11" diameter, red and white marbled with red trim. *Courtesy of David T. Pikul, The Chuctanunda Antique Co.* $150-200.

European salt box, blue and white chicken wire pattern with red trim, wooden lid, and French lettering. *Courtesy of Susan Curran, Snow Leopard Antiques.* $275-325.

European coffee biggin, 10 1/2" tall, gray mottled with black trim. *Courtesy of David T. Pikul, The Chuctanunda Antique Co.* $100-250.

European canister set, white with blue and orange feather pattern. *Courtesy of David T. Pikul, The Chuctanunda Antique Co.* $375-450.

American bundt pan, cobalt blue and white marbled. *Courtesy of Stan & MaryAnn Szambelan.* $200-250.

American cream carrier, 6" tall, gray mottled with wire and wooden handle. *Courtesy of Betty Duquet.* $125-150.

European triple-soap laundry rack with blue and white chicken wire pattern and German lettering for sand, soap, and soda. Unusual example in that the cups hang by hooks rather than sitting in rack. *Courtesy of Susan Curran, Snow Leopard Antiques.* $300-375.

European (Dutch) wall-hung three-cup laundry rack, blue and white mottled pattern. *Courtesy of David T. Pikul, The Chuctanunda Antique Co.* $150-200.

European body pitcher, 16" tall, rare red and white mottled. *Courtesy of David T. Pikul, The Chuctanunda Antique Co.* $400-500.

## Chapter Four
# Enameled Ware Graphic Designs

Could there be anything more striking than an enameled coffee biggin adorned with garlands of roses or a canister set displaying bold and playful checks? For many devoted collectors, the graphic designs on antique enameled ware are the most remarkable feature.

The use of eye-catching graphic designs on enameled ware is of European origin. Utility, of course, was the catalyst in the development of a porcelain enamel finish to be used over iron and sheet steel, but the old European studios that perfected the art also endeavored to create some of the aesthetic appeal long associated with decorative enamel work. Toward that end, during the late 1800s artists were employed in Europe to hand decorate a wide variety of items intended for household use.

Initially European studios produced enameled ware in white to provide a cost-effective and practical alternative to ceramics. It was only natural that decorations would soon follow. For example, a stylized blue floral motif was highly favored in Germany and Northern European countries, especially Holland, where blue and white Delft tiles had long been used in the home as a decorative design element and symbol of cleanliness. In addition to floral graphics, sailboats and windmill scenes done in blue on white enameled ware were also produced.

European kettle, 5 1/2" tall, red and white checkered design. *Courtesy of David T. Pikul, The Chuctanunda Antique Co.* $150-200.

As expected, floral and nature motifs also followed period styles. In Germany gifted artists adorned many enameled ware pieces with delicate, simple roses—a motif long associated with a rural lifestyle and reminiscent of the Biedermier period (circa 1815 through the 1840s) which had long-lasting influence on furniture styles as well as interior design. Naturalistic designs such as wildflowers, birds, and butterflies also appeared on numerous pieces produced in Germany, France, and other European countries.

The French, too, were widely recognized for their Rococo style decorations including graceful, petit garlands of roses which were often combined with thin striping or gilt trimwork. The French also excelled at producing fine examples of enameled ware with Art Nouveau graphics such as stylized flowers.

During the early 1900s floral and nature motifs persisted but by the late 1920s and during the 1930s Art Deco, with its geometric designs, was everywhere apparent on European enameled ware. Stripes and checkered patterns in vibrant hues were used to adorn everything from utensil racks to handy little match boxes.

While anonymous artists did indeed hand paint enameled ware produced abroad during the late 1800s, by the turn of the century this practice proved a financial drain for many studios. Steps were taken to cut costs and change the manner in which graphic designs were applied. As a result, stamps were put into use to outline a design that was then filled in by hand. Tissue paper transfers, steel engravings, silk screening, and decals were also in widespread use at enameling shops during the 1910s, 1920s, and 1930s. These methods, however, still required a certain degree of artistic skill and hands-on work.

Along with the stunning graphics that were used, many items called for lettering to proclaim their intended use. Canister sets, salt boxes, match boxes, potholder containers, towel racks, and so on were routinely lettered with stencils, decals, or hand-lettering. And while the language displayed can often times be an indication of the country of origin, there are exceptions to this. For example, Austria, Belgium, and Czechoslovakia produced enameled ware specifically for the French market, complete with French lettering.

And what of American-made enameled ware in regard to graphic designs? During the late 1800s those items made for the middle class Victorian dining room were adorned with floral and nature motifs produced via decals. Most of these same pieces, as previously discussed, had elegant pewter or nickel-plate trim. For example, an 1886 Milwaukee, Wisconsin, hardware catalog included a handsome coffee pot decorated with a nature scene of a stork in a bayou. Also included was a teapot with a floral decoration consisting of a wreath of violets. While both were advertised as being hand-painted, this indirectly referred to the original artwork from which the decal was designed.

Graphic designs on enameled ware did not reach the level of importance in the United States that they did in Europe. Not until the 1930s did several U.S. manufacturers routinely use decals on their kitchenware items. Stencils, too, were used, especially on advertising premiums and promotional give-away items.

We have already discussed the fact that the process of creating enameled ware is today a lost art; add to that those pieces (many are one of a kind) adorned with graphic designs and they become highly collectible artistic treasures.

European coffee biggin, 10 1/2" tall, red and white mini-print design with black trim. *Courtesy of David T. Pikul, The Chuctanunda Antique Co.* $250-295.

*Opposite page:*
Large European coffee biggin, double handles, white with yellow shading and floral graphic design. *Courtesy of Pamela DeBisschop.*

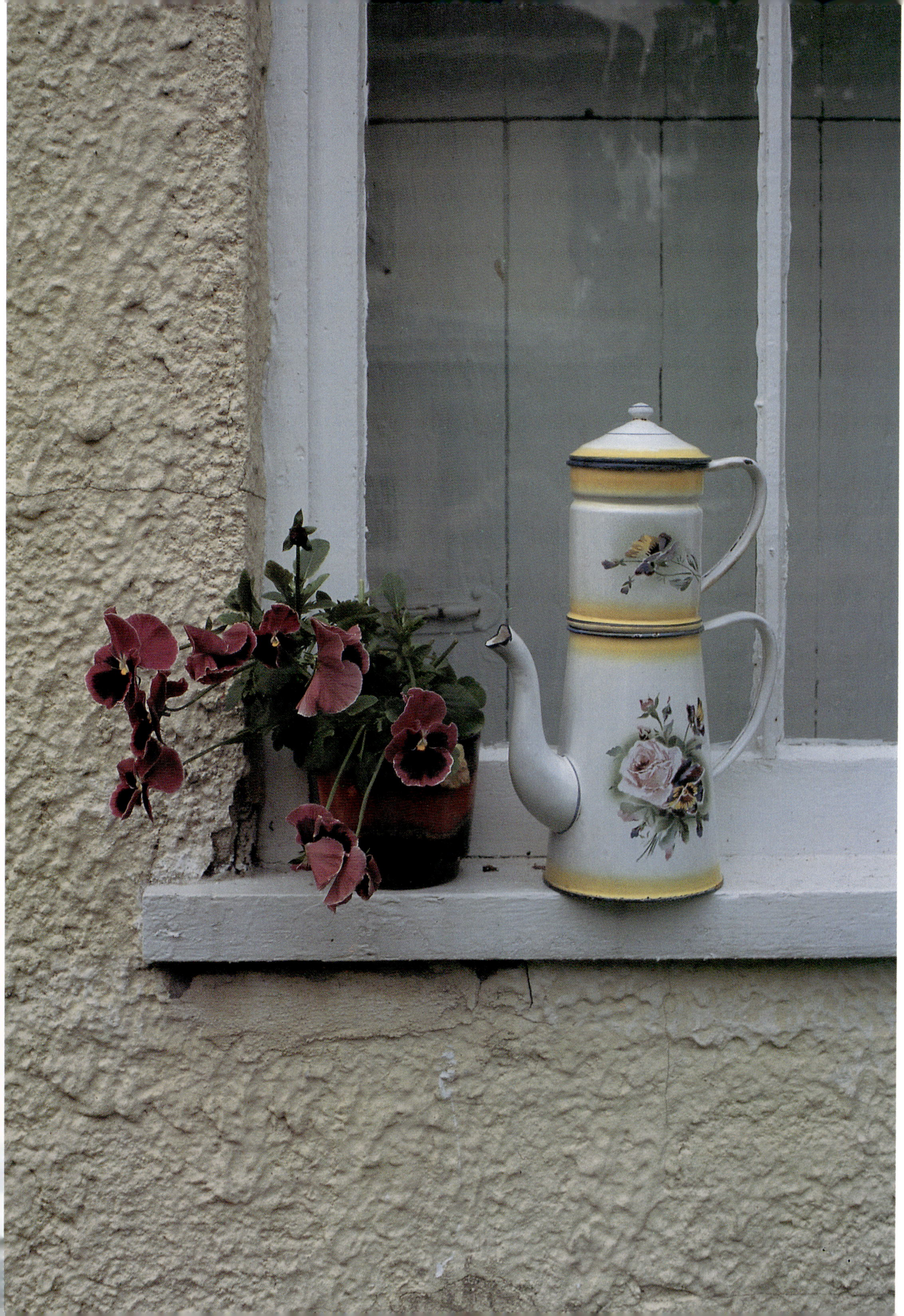

American teapot, 11" tall, white with metal trim and a graphic design of a stork in the bayou. *Courtesy of Betty Duquet.* $350-400.

European body pitcher, 16" tall, blue and white shading with raised floral design. *Courtesy of David T. Pikul, The Chuctanunda Antique Co.* $300-375.

European coffee carrier (9" tall) and coffee biggin (10 1/2" tall). White with red check design and red trim. *Courtesy of David T. Pikul, The Chuctanunda Antique Co.* Coffee carrier $150-175; biggin $250-295.

European wall-hung three-cup laundry set, red with white graphic design and French lettering. *Courtesy of David T. Pikul, The Chuctanunda Antique Co.* $225-275.

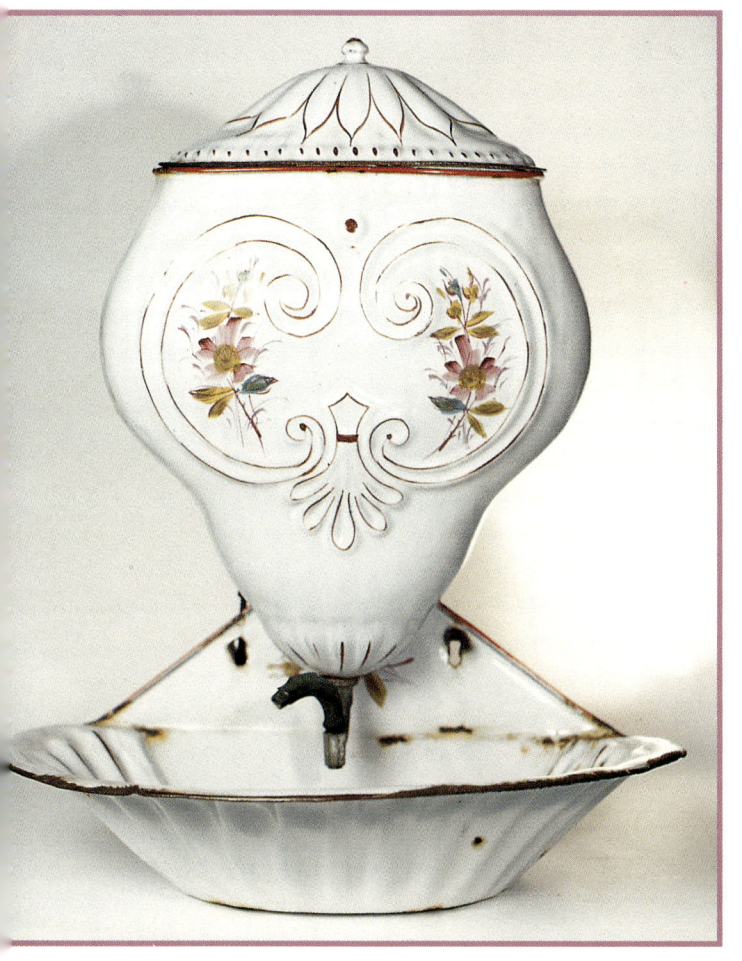

European teapot, 5 1/2" tall, pink and white shading with banded graphic design. *Courtesy of David T. Pikul, The Chuctanunda Antique Co.* $250-300.

Early European lavabo, tear-drop shaped tank and scalloped basin. White with ornate floral graphic design and red trim. *Courtesy of David T. Pikul, The Chuctanunda Antique Co.* $500-700.

European coffee carrier, 9" tall, white with floral graphics and blue design. *Courtesy of David T. Pikul, The Chuctanunda Antique Co.* $125-175.

European (Austrian) teapot, 6" tall with air-brushed floral stencil design. Marked "Elite." *Courtesy of David T. Pikul, The Chuctanunda Antique Co.* $150-175.

European pitcher, 10" tall, cobalt blue with white floral design. *Courtesy of Betty Duquet.* $125-150.

European (probably made in Austria) footed colander and funnel, white with red checkered graphic design. Marked "B&B." *Courtesy of David T. Pikul, The Chuctanunda Antique Co.* Colander $150-175; funnel $75-95.

European coffee biggin, 10 1/2" tall, unusual cobalt blue and white graphic design with red trim. *Courtesy of David T. Pikul, The Chuctanunda Antique Co.* $250-295.

European pail, 8" tall, blue and white shaded with large floral (roses) graphic design. *Courtesy of David T. Pikul, The Chuctanunda Antique Co.* $250-325.

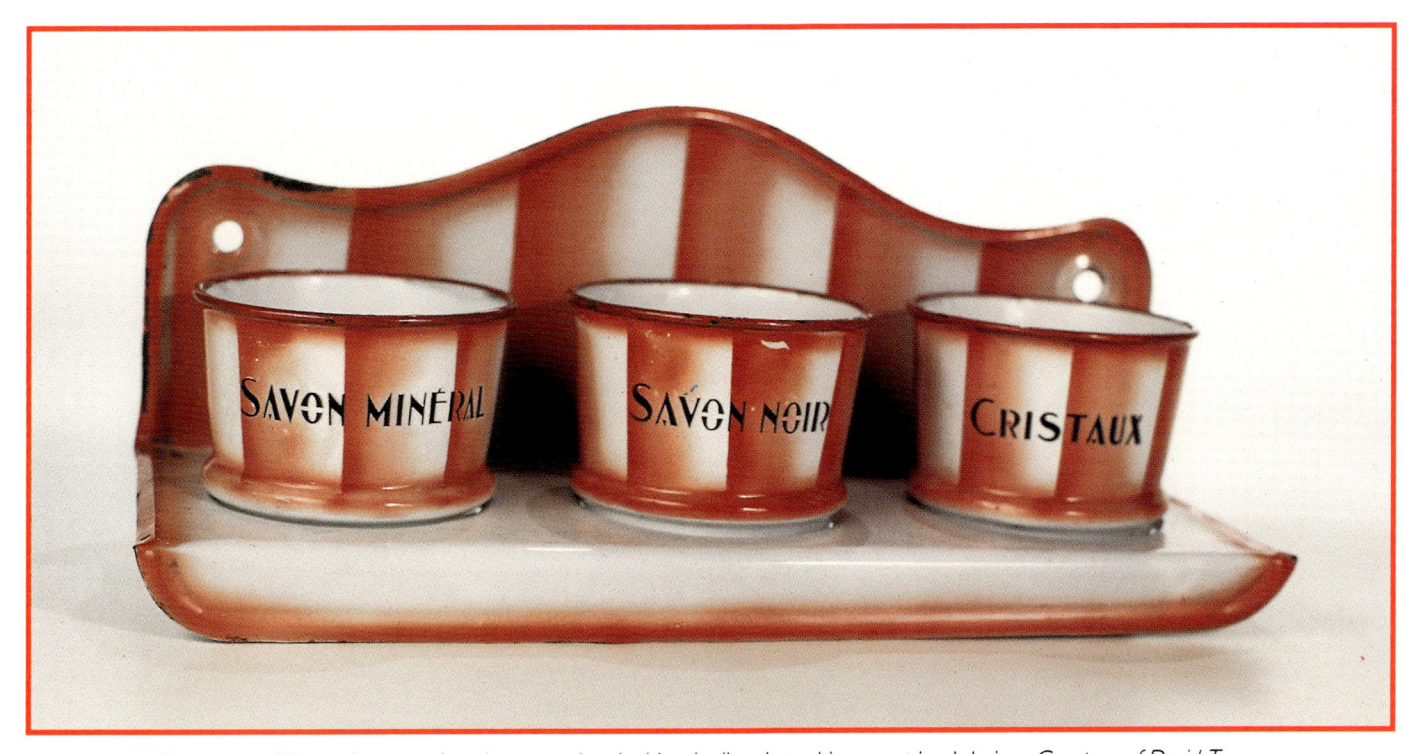

European wall-hung three-cup laundry set, red and white shading that achieves a striped design. *Courtesy of David T. Pikul, The Chuctanunda Antique Co.* $250-300.

133

Large European coffee biggin, double handles, rare blue and white droopy check design with red trim. *Courtesy of Susan Curran, Snow Leopard Antiques.* $500-600.

European (Austrian) teapot, 5 1/2" tall, Art Deco graphic design. Teapot marked "Elite." *Courtesy of Betty Duquet.* $125-175.

European (Austrian) syrup pitcher, 5" tall, yellow and white graphic design. Marked "Elite." *Courtesy of David T. Pikul, The Chuctanunda Antique Co.* $150-225.

European wall-hung salt box, red and white shading with Art Deco graphic design and French lettering. Marked "AUBECO." *Courtesy of David T. Pikul, The Chuctanunda Antique Co.* $175-250.

European canister set, red with black and white banded design and French lettering. *Courtesy of David T. Pikul, The Chuctanunda Antique Co.* $450-600.

European coffee carriers (Austrian), 9 1/2" tall, white with blue and red graphic designs. Marked "Elite." *Courtesy of David T. Pikul, The Chuctanunda Antique Co.* $150-200 each.

European coffee biggin, 11" tall, rare combination of mottled pattern and floral graphic design. *Courtesy of Susan Curran, Snow Leopard Antiques.* $300-400.

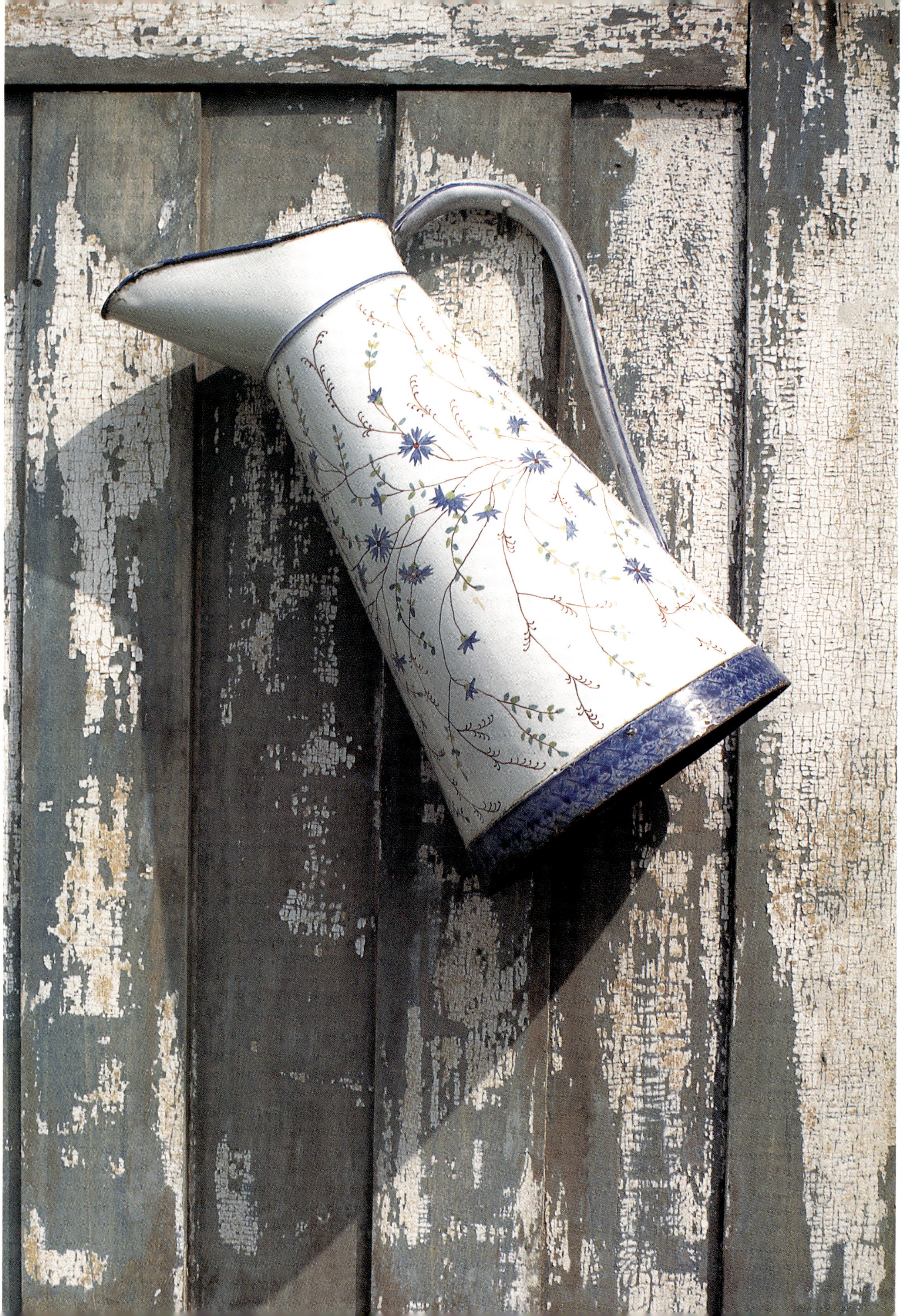

European canister set, pink with unusual graphic design on the top half of each canister, French lettering. *Courtesy of Susan Curran, Snow Leopard Antiques.* $400-500.

European souvenir pitcher, 7" tall, scenic graphic design. *Courtesy of Susan Curran, Snow Leopard Antiques.* $200-275.

European chocolate pot, 11" tall, rare item, white with floral graphics. *Courtesy of Susan Curran, Snow Leopard Antiques.* $375-450.

*Opposite page:*
European body pitcher, white with blue trim and delicate floral design. *Courtesy of Pamela DeBisschop.*

European canister set, matches salt box in previous photo. *Courtesy of Susan Curran, Snow Leopard Antiques.* $400-500.

European wall-hung salt box, yellow stripes and blue floral design with French lettering. *Courtesy of Susan Curran, Snow Leopard Antiques.* $175-250.

European coffee biggin, 9 1/2" tall, rare gray-blue color with Dutch figures and red and white trim. *Courtesy of David T. Pikul, The Chuctanunda Antique Co.* $325-375.

European water pitcher, 10 1/2" tall, extremely rare all-over floral graphic design. *Courtesy of Susan Curran, Snow Leopard Antiques.* $650-800.

European wall-hung potholder basket, white with blue windmill scene and German lettering. *Courtesy of Susan Curran, Snow Leopard Antiques.* $200-275.

European canister set with blue stripes, garlands of roses, and French lettering. Marked "B&B." Quite possibly made in Austria for the French market. *Courtesy of Susan Curran, Snow Leopard Antiques.* $500-600.

European utensil rack with tools, white with blue trim and nature-inspired scenic design. *Courtesy of Susan Curran, Snow Leopard Antiques.* $300-400.

Large European coffee biggin, 12" tall, double handles, blue and white shaded with pansy floral design. *Courtesy of Susan Curran, Snow Leopard Antiques.* $350-500.

*Below:* European wall-hung laundry set, brown with white air-brushed stencil design and French lettering. *Courtesy of Susan Curran, Snow Leopard Antiques.* $275-350.

American coffee pot, 11" tall, white and pink with floral graphics and metal trim. *Courtesy of Susan Curran, Snow Leopard Antiques.* $250-325.

European pitcher, 6" tall, scenic design. *Courtesy of Susan Curran, Snow Leopard Antiques.* $200-275.

European teapot, 6 1/2" tall, red with floral graphic design. *Courtesy of Susan Curran, Snow Leopard Antiques.* $175-250.

European oval platter, white with floral graphics and gilt trim. *Courtesy of Pamela DeBisschop.*

American teapot, 13" tall, white with metal trim and floral graphic design. *Courtesy of Susan Curran, Snow Leopard Antiques.* $200-300.

European measuring pitcher, 9" tall, red and white checkered graphic design. *Courtesy of Susan Curran, Snow Leopard Antiques.* $275-350.

European wall-hung salt box, white with pale blue shading, floral design, and German lettering. *Courtesy of David T. Pikul, The Chuctanunda Antique Co.* $200-275.

European coffee biggin, 10 1/2" tall, orange and red shading with band of checks. *Courtesy of David T. Pikul, The Chuctanunda Antique Co.* $275-325.

European teapot, 4 1/2" tall, light blue with black checkered band. Marked "Germany." *Courtesy of David T. Pikul, The Chuctanunda Antique Co.* $100-125.

European canister set, white with red striping, floral bands, and French lettering. *Courtesy of David T. Pikul, The Chuctanunda Antique Co.* $500-600.

European coffee pot, 9" tall, white with cobalt blue graphic design. *Courtesy of Stephen Smith, Foundation Antiques.* $125-175.

European teapot, 5 1/2" tall, red and white with Art Deco graphic design. Marked "AUBECO." *Courtesy of David T. Pikul, The Chuctanunda Antique Co.* $175-225.

European wall-hung salt box, white with floral design and French lettering. *Courtesy of David T. Pikul, The Chuctanunda Antique Co.* $175-225.

Large European coffee biggin, 12" tall, white with subtle shading and floral graphic design. *Courtesy of David T. Pikul, The Chuctanunda Antique Co.* $400-500.

*Below:* European canister set, rare red and white droopy check with French lettering. *Courtesy of Susan Curran, Snow Leopard Antiques.* $500-600.

European syrup pitcher (4" tall) and teapot (9" tall), both blue with raised floral graphic design. *Courtesy of David T. Pikul, The Chuctanunda Antique Co.* Syrup pitcher $175-225; teapot $200-250.

European coffee pot, 9" tall, white with yellow band and duck design. *Courtesy of David T. Pikul, The Chuctanunda Antique Co.* $200-275.

European utensil rack with single tool, orange with black and white checkered design. *Courtesy of David T. Pikul, The Chuctanunda Antique Co.* $300-375.

European coffee biggin, 10 1/2" tall, "French blue" with blue and white checkered band. *Courtesy of David T. Pikul, The Chuctanunda Antique Co.* $250-300.

European body pitcher, 15" tall, blue and white shading with diagonal floral graphic design. *Courtesy of David T. Pikul, The Chuctanunda Antique Co.* $250-325.

European pitcher and basin, white with blue and orange graphic design. *Courtesy of David T. Pikul, The Chuctanunda Antique Co.* $300-400.

American teapot, 7 1/2" tall, white with metal trim and floral graphics. *Courtesy of David T. Pikul, The Chuctanunda Antique Co.* $300-400.

European salt box, very unique shape, white with "French blue" band, gilt trim, and decorative design. *Courtesy of David T. Pikul, The Chuctanunda Antique Co.* $175-250.

European syrup pitcher, 5" tall, red and white check design. Marked "B&B." *Courtesy of David T. Pikul, The Chuctanunda Antique Co.* $150-175.

European body pitcher, 15" tall, rare red and white droopy check design. *Courtesy of Stan & MaryAnn Szambelan.* $400-500.

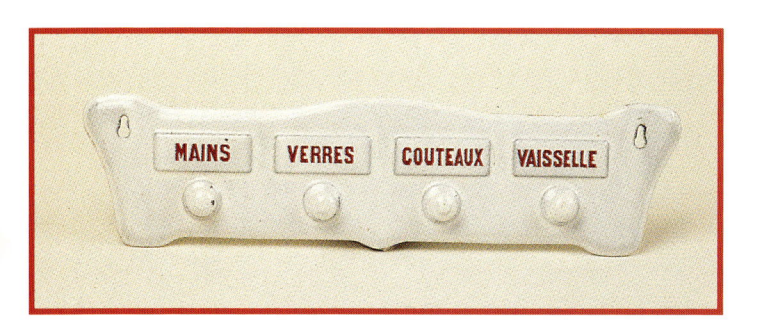

European towel rack, white with red lettering in French. *Courtesy of David T. Pikul, The Chuctanunda Antique Co.* $150-175.

European footed bowl, 4" tall, white with floral design, circa late 1800s. *Courtesy of David T. Pikul, The Chuctanunda Antique Co.* $125-175.

European (Austrian) teapot, 6 1/2" tall, air-brushed stencil design with black trim. Marked "Elite." *Courtesy of David T. Pikul, The Chuctanunda Antique Co.* $175-225.

European coffee pot, 10" tall, rare pink coloring with floral graphic design. *Courtesy of David T. Pikul, The Chuctanunda Antique Co.* $300-400.

European coffee biggin, white with blue shading and pansy floral design. *Courtesy of David T. Pikul, The Chuctanunda Antique Co.* $250-295.

European salt box, large cobalt blue and white checks, wooden lid, French lettering. *Courtesy of David T. Pikul, The Chuctanunda Antique Co.* $300-375

European teapot, 6" tall, white with floral graphic design. *Courtesy of David T. Pikul, The Chuctanunda Antique Co.* $150-200.

European milk pail, 11" tall, red and white checkered design. *Courtesy of David T. Pikul, The Chuctanunda Antique Co.* $250-300.

European canister set, cobalt blue and white checkered design. *Courtesy of Pamela DeBisschop.* $500-600.

151

European teapot, 4 1/2" tall, red with black trim and black and white checkered band. *Courtesy of David T. Pikul, The Chuctanunda Antique Co.* $150-200.

European measuring pitcher, 9" tall, white with blue shading and rose floral design. *Courtesy of David T. Pikul, The Chuctanunda Antique Co.* $200-300.

European plates and cups, white with red trim, floral sprays, and personalized lettering. *Courtesy of Pamela DeBisschop.* $150-200.

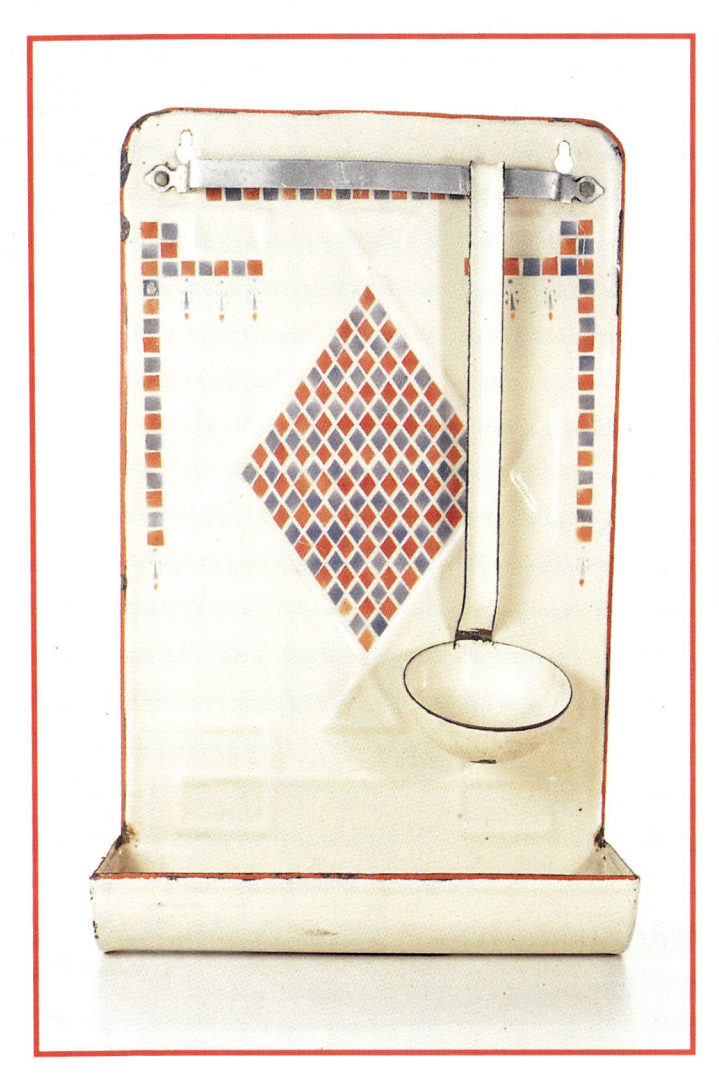

European utensil rack, white with red trim and red and blue diamond design. *Courtesy of David T. Pikul, The Chuctanunda Antique Co.* $275-325.

European (Austrian) teapot, 5" tall, air-brushed floral stencil design. Marked "Elite." *Courtesy of Betty Duquet.* $150-175.

European syrup pitcher, 8" tall, white with red stripes and floral design. *Courtesy of David T. Pikul, The Chuctanunda Antique Co.* $175-225.

European body pitcher, 15" tall, red and white shading with fuchsia floral graphic design and gilt trim. *Courtesy of Ellen M. Plante.* $325-400.

European cups and saucers, white with blue Art Deco graphic designs. *Courtesy of David T. Pikul, The Chuctanunda Antique Co.* $75-100.

European wall-hung flour box, 11" tall, white with a wooden lid, floral graphics, and German lettering. *Courtesy of Susan Curran, Snow Leopard Antiques.* $300-375.

Large European (French) coffee biggin with double handles, white with rare commemorative scenes depicting a bridge and a Ferris wheel. *Courtesy of David T. Pikul, The Chuctanunda Antique Co.* $600-700.

European wall-hung three-cup laundry rack, rare cobalt blue with ornate German script for sand, soap, and soda. *Courtesy of David T. Pikul, The Chuctanunda Antique Co.* $300-400.

European utensil rack with tools, white with red stripes and checks. *Courtesy of Stan & MaryAnn Szambelan.* $225-300.

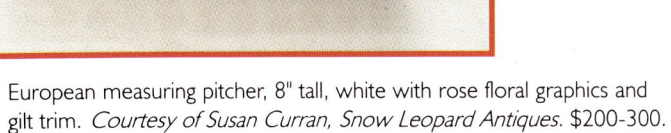

European coffee biggin, 9 1/2" tall, white with petite rose floral graphic design. *Courtesy of David T. Pikul, The Chuctanunda Antique Co.* $300-400.

European measuring pitcher, 8" tall, white with rose floral graphics and gilt trim. *Courtesy of Susan Curran, Snow Leopard Antiques.* $200-300.

European body pitcher, 15" tall, blue and white air-brushed floral stencil design. *Courtesy of Susan Curran, Snow Leopard Antiques.* $300-400.

Large European coffee biggin, 13" tall, double handles, cream color with stylized graphic design and gilt trim. *Courtesy of David T. Pikul, The Chuctanunda Antique Co.* $300-400.

European coffee biggin, 10 1/2" tall, light blue and white check design. *Courtesy of David T. Pikul, The Chuctanunda Antique Co.* $275-325.

European coffee biggin, 11" tall, red with black Art Deco graphic design. *Courtesy of David T. Pikul, The Chuctanunda Antique Co.* $300-400.

European covered pot, 12" diameter, white with blue shading and rose floral graphics. *Courtesy of David T. Pikul, The Chuctanunda Antique Co.* $200-250.

European body pitcher, orange and white droopy check design. *Courtesy of Pamela DeBisschop.*

European wall-hung three-cup laundry set, blue and white check design, French lettering. *Courtesy of David T. Pikul, The Chuctanunda Antique Co.* $200-300.

European canister set, red with white diamond graphic design. *Courtesy of David T. Pikul, The Chuctanunda Antique Co.* $400-500.

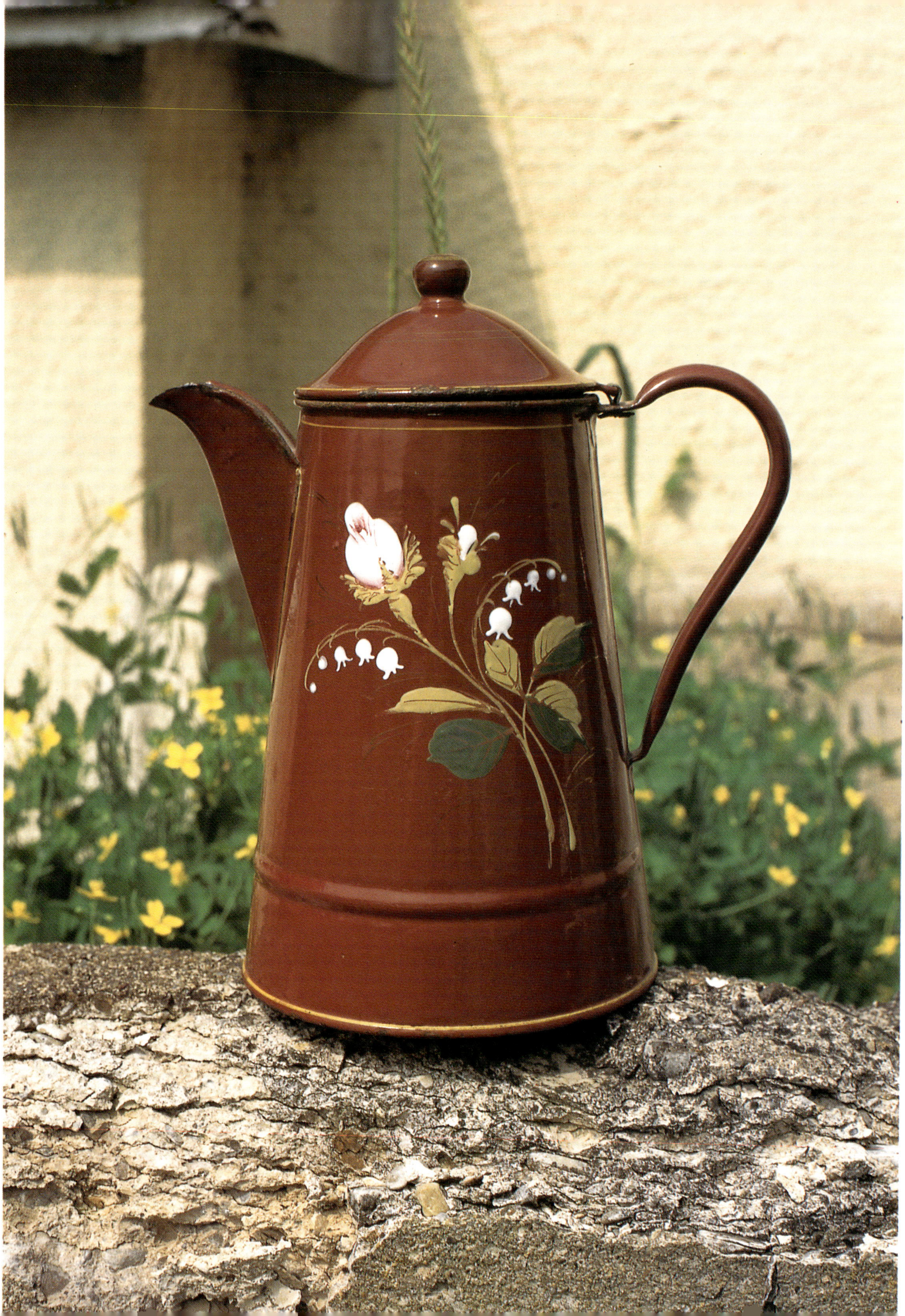

# Chapter Five
# Addictive Properties

When discussing the enameled ware produced between the late 1800s and 1940s the collector of course is concerned with condition, pricing, provenance, and caring for a collection.

Condition can generally be thought of in terms of mint, near mint, good, and poor. It is unrealistic to expect to build a sizable collection entirely of mint pieces. Enameled ware was intended for constant use; small chips are often to be expected and will not detract greatly from the beauty and value of an otherwise wonderful piece. With this in mind, consider "mint" as describing a piece that looks as if it's never been used. "Near mint" refers to pieces with small chips only—no other notable signs of damage or use. "Good condition" may imply a larger chip or two, some rust, but at the very least a presentable side. "Poor condition" can mean large chips, rust, missing pieces, or extensive crazing. Naturally you should buy the very best you can afford, not necessarily for investment potential, but for enameled ware's aesthetic appeal and decorative value.

Pricing, as mentioned in the Foreword of this book, is determined by so many variables that ultimately you the collector must determine what you are willing to pay for any given piece. Remember that condition, rarity (in terms of color, item, decorative designs) and even specific regions of the country influence price. Add to that global popularity, for enameled ware is collected in Great Britain, Japan, and throughout Europe as well as in North America, and prices will reflect supply and demand. American antiques dealers specializing in European enameled ware have seen the availability of enameled ware shrink considerably due to increased demand abroad and competition from other foreign markets.

There are clues to determining the provenance of any given piece of enameled ware. Older examples made of iron are noticeably heavier than sheet steel examples. Check for rivets and seams which were used in construction early on by many companies in assembling a piece. Become familiar with colors; many can be associated with a specific company or time frame. Older examples of enameled ware tend to have two or more coats of enamel rather than the singular coat found on modern-day reproductions. Graphic designs often reflect stylistic periods. Markings are also a good indication of age as well as country of origin or manufacturer. A manufacturer's trademark may have been applied with a stamp, or later, a paper label. European enameled ware exported to the United States often has the country of origin marked on the bottom or a manufacturer name. For example, pieces marked "Elite" are Austrian while "Paragon" denote a German manufacturer. European examples tnat are today purchased abroad by antiques dealers and brought back to the United States may or may not be marked. Those that are, however, are usually stamped with the firm's name and/or a logo. Sometimes an artist marked a piece with their initials.

You'll naturally want to care for your enameled ware collection by dusting and washing with soap and water regularly. For very dirty or soiled pieces oven cleaner has been used with great success, but test on an inconspicuous area first. Naval Jelly, Zud cleanser, and Whink are all good at removing rust. Bleach can be used for whitening and for removing stubborn stains such as residual coffee and tea. Chemical combinations can be deadly, so read all labels carefully. Work with one chemical on one operation at a time. For example, don't let rust remover work on one piece, while using bleach on another. Chemicals can react—even when dumped down the drain. Items intended for display only can be spray waxed to maintain shine and protect the piece from dust and dirt.

*Opposite page:*
European coffee pot, brown with floral graphic design. *Courtesy of Pamela DeBisschop.*

# BIBLIOGRAPHY

## BOOKS

Barlow, Ronald S. *Victorian Houseware, Hardware and Kitchenware.* El Cajon, California: Windmill Publishing Company, 1992.

Bishop, Christina. *Miller's Collecting Kitchenware.* London, England: Miller's (an imprint of Reed Books), 1995.

Greguire, Helen. *The Collector's Encyclopedia of Granite Ware.* Paducah, Kentucky: Collector Books, 1990.

_____. *The Collector's Encyclopedia of Granite Ware Book II.* Paducah, Kentucky: Collector Books, 1993.

Kate-von Eicken, Brigitte ten. *L'ÉMail dans la maison.* Paris, France: Armand Colin, 1992.

Lifshey, Earl. *The Housewares Story.* Chicago, Illinois: National Housewares Manufacturers Association, 1973.

*Montgomery Ward & Co. Spring & Summer 1895 Catalog.* New York, New York: Dover Publications, Inc., unabridged facsimile published 1969.

Plante, Ellen M. *The American Kitchen 1700 to the Present.* New York, New York: Facts on File, Inc., 1995.

*Sears, Roebuck and Company Fall 1900 Catalog.* Northfield, Illinois: Digest Books, Inc., facsimile published in 1970.

Vogelzang, Vernagene and Evelyn Welch. *Graniteware: Collector's Guide with Prices.* Lombard, Illinois: Wallace-Homestead Book Company, 1981.

_____. *Granite Ware: Collector's Guide with Prices Book II.* Radnor, Pennsylvania, 1986.

## PERIODICALS

"French Enamelware," *Country Living*, February 1997: pg. 76.

Johnson, Julia Claiborne. "Enamelware," *Martha Stewart Living*, June/July 1994: pg. 35.

Plante, Ellen M. "Enamel Imports—Old-World Kitchen Collectibles," *Country Collectibles*, Fall 1995: pg. 32.

_____. "Hold Everything," *Country Living*, June 1997: pg. 80.

Smith, Scott. "Graniteware," *Bon Appétit*, September 1992: pg. 26.

Weiss, Gloria K. "Graniteware," *Country Living*, November 1996: pg. 20.

European match box and salt box, rare red and white droopy check design with French lettering in blue. *Courtesy of Susan Curran, Snow Leopard Antiques.* Match box $250-300; salt box $275-350.